Miracles

and

Parables

what narrative icons are saying

Mary Jane Miller

Miracles and Parables what narrative icons are saying
by Mary Jane Miller
www.millericons.com
All text and paintings by Mary Jane Miller.

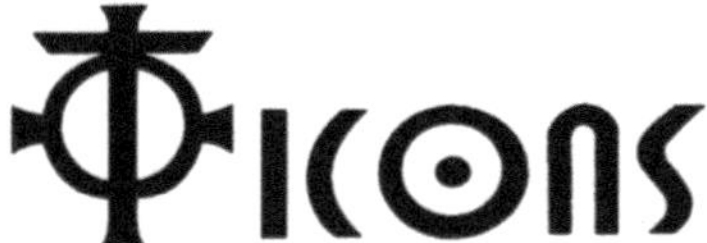

ISBN 979-8-9886283-6-1

Introduction

Miracles and Parables is a small book designed to address new attitude: that Jesus the man and Christ the consciousness 'are' and are not the same. Jesus lived and taught us through signs and miracles. He showed us what it looks like to be fully human by walking among us. Christ on the other hand is the spirit of God manifested first in Jesus the man and now Divine energy dispersed and made accessible for all of humanity.

Mary Jane is respectful of the iconography tradition and knowledgeable of its long history but feels free to challenge the male-dominated church landscape of today's theology. The text and image are uniquely formatted. Because an image is without words its impact is gentler, our response may be emotional without words. With the added descriptions and history the iconography comes alive in a special dynamic way.

Our world is full of energy and changes constantly with new perspectives on spiritual meaning and prayer. Mary Jane is one of a growing community of female iconographers whose voice is using text and imagery to reveal and share insights and deeper discernment about what it means to live a spiritual existence. Even if you do not already appreciate religious imagery, thisbook is worth the read. The fascinating iconography tradition and its visual language will speak to you and draw you into their ancient world of noesis.

Through Mary Jane Miller's iconography, a fresh vision of faith has and continues to inform and shape spiritual people. A parable is a simple tale about a common subject that illustrates a more profound truth and in this case through image. For Jesus, miracles and parables illustrated the presence of God the Creator. The stories are sensible, earthly incidents that convey an ideal heavenly meaning and valuable moral lesson. The Sacred Art of painting an icon is a captivating blend of modernity and spirituality.

Miracles and Parables is a 44-page introduction to narrative iconography, it incorporates 30 full-color icons, all original works by Mary Jane Miller using a mixture of egg yolk and ancient dirt. She juxtaposed the images with text that included history, religious context, and her reflections. The iconography combines inspired meditation and prayer to stimulate startling conclusions hidden in the images.

Each icon in the collection is meticulously crafted using earth pigments and carefully layered to create a flawless masterpiece. The egg tempera technique beautifully captures the Earth's essence and organic life while melding with ancient Biblical imagery.

Drawing inspiration from the masterpieces of Byzantine iconographers in Russia, Greece, and Eastern Europe, the collection of works called Miracles and Parables becomes a testament to the rich artistic heritage of these regions in a contemporary format.

There are many ways to appreciate the visual language of icons. Their theological interpretation and message, their symbolism and layers of meaning, their historical and cultural story, the meditative and symbolic way in which they are created, and the artistic technique and practice they represent.

This collection "Miracles and Parables" was exhibited in the Teryl Viner Gallery in the Community Church in Vero Beach, Florida in 2024 and 2025.

Forward

by Sy Brontide

I met Mary Jane in 2021 in a magical town called San Miguel Allende, tucked among the mountains of central Mexico. She introduced me to the captivating and mysterious world of iconography. Before then, other than a passing appreciation for the artwork on the walls of various cathedrals I had visited during my travels, I had zero interest in icons or their creation. Little did I know, there was a feisty, gringa iconographer living a few doors down who was about to knock my childhood Jesus right off his shelf and back into my life.

And so I was introduced to the world of iconography, to Mary Jane, and to her Jesus. I soon learned that there was much more to iconography than pretty pictures on the walls of religious institutions. I could clearly see that Mary Jane had deep respect for the ancient tradition of iconography and for biblical religious tradition, as well as in preserving and passing them on. It was also apparent that she was unafraid to examine and question the long-held beliefs of those traditions.

Our discussions ranged far and wide, from the symbolism of angel antennae and floating donkeys, to 5th dimension possibilities, to the meaning of dreams, and the attributes of the divine. Nothing was off limits. It was clear that Mary Jane's Jesus occupied a much larger box than anyone's I had ever met. And because of her fearless questioning, she was constantly poking holes in that box, expanding it and letting the light in. I found myself re-examining my conclusions and experiences with Bible-based religion, with art as spiritual practice, and with the divine.

Since then, I've had the pleasure of a front row seat to the creation of several of Mary Jane's books on iconography. I've been a sounding board and editor, and a curious observer of her artistic and creative practice. And what I've learned is this: all of Mary Jane's work comes from a place of love. A fierce love for Jesus, for the tradition of iconography, and for this precious planet Earth. And because of this love and out of this love, she is willing to question and expose the areas where we may have limited the divine, where growth is needed, and where perhaps we can do better.

Regardless of what has prompted you to pick up a book like this, I invite you to crack open the windows and doors of your mind and allow a journey of possibility; to a world of symbolism, imagery, subtext, mystery, and wonder; to allow yourself to contemplate and question things you may have thought were absolute. Because if you do, perhaps like me, you will not only be surprised and delighted, but also changed.

I know meeting Mary Jane on that cobbled street ironically named Sacred Heart, was no accident. And although my Jesus is now back on his shelf, albeit a less dusty shelf and one closer to the window, there is a new richness to my artistic and spiritual practice for having entertained the questions and contemplated the possibilities and what ifs.

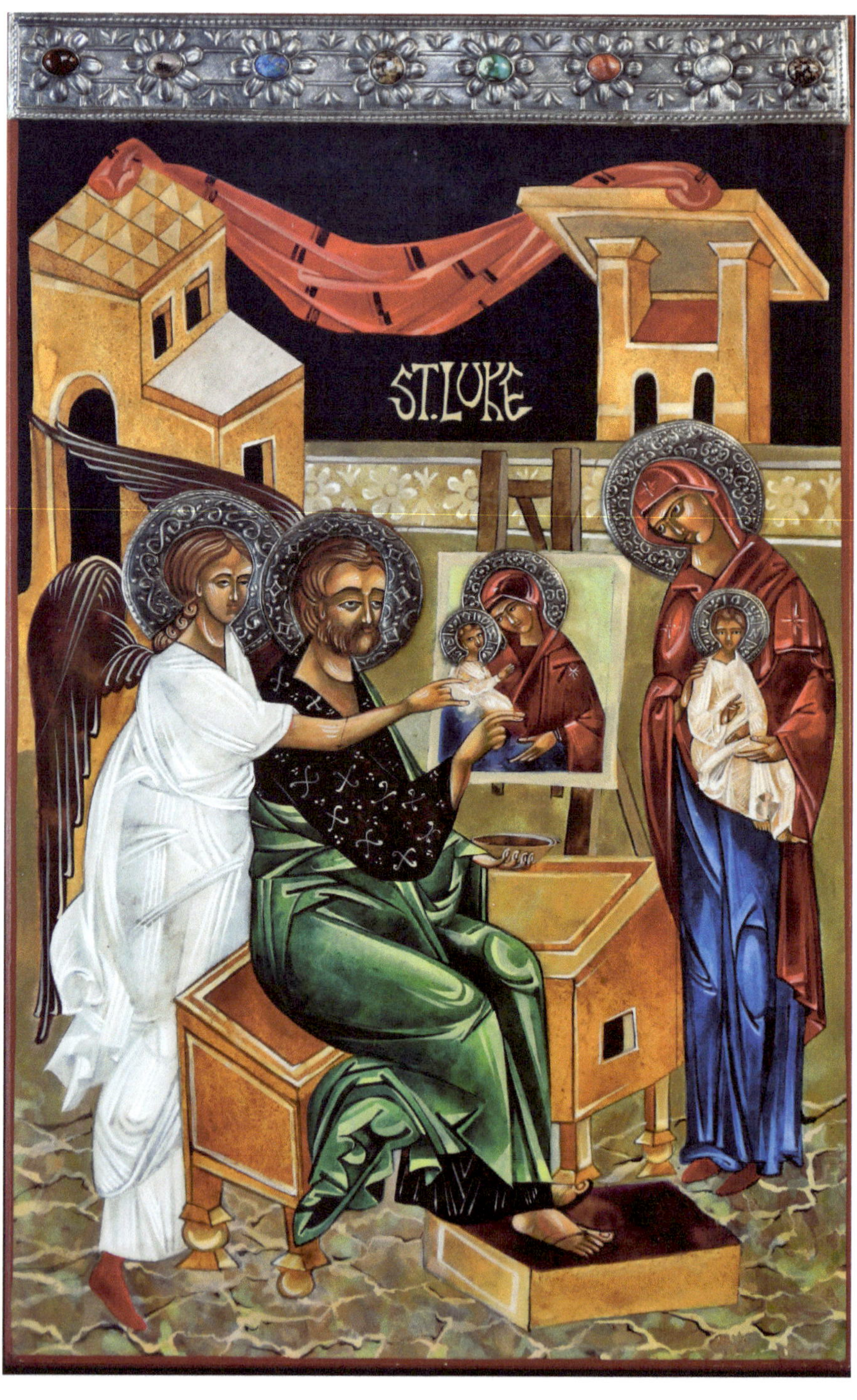
ST.LUKE

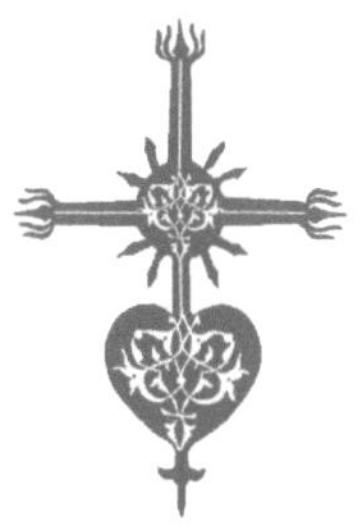

Saint Luke Painting an Icon

This classic icon of St Luke painting the Virgin Mary is the icon of icons for iconographers, it defines the iconographer's relationship that inspires our desire to paint, how it works, and why. Icon design and message do not portray static reality. We avoid references to historical locations and time of day. There is no light source or shadows.

The activity of St Luke's painting is happening on three levels and in three dimensions of time, outside of past, present, and future. The first level depicts St Luke seated at an easel painting or writing an icon on a wooden panel. It is a normal activity happening in any painter's studio, at any time or place. The miraculous apparition of Mary and Jesus represents the second level. This vision comes to him as an actual historical event. St Luke captures what he sees in the vision with paint and brush, its meaning and significance. The event has already happened and is documented in the bible. Iconographers use scripture for the icon's design and message.

Notice the translation from the apparition to the board. St Luke has consciously or subconsciously altered what he perceives. The third level is the inspiration received from the angel. We cannot physically touch and be sure of spiritual presence. What feels like an angelic presence is without a doubt real and assists in much of what we do. We experience an intuitive awareness that is not of this world, yet this same metaphysical presence sustains us and gives ideas, epiphanies, and moments of ah-ha that change everything.

Painting narrative icons remind me that spirit is present everywhere at all times, whether known or unknown. God is constant but history and change are limitless. Iconographers are aware of the physical, historical, and spiritual dimensions without division on three levels.

ST LUKE IS NOT ALONE AS HE PAINTS,
HE IS ASSISTED AS WE ARE ALL ASSISTED.

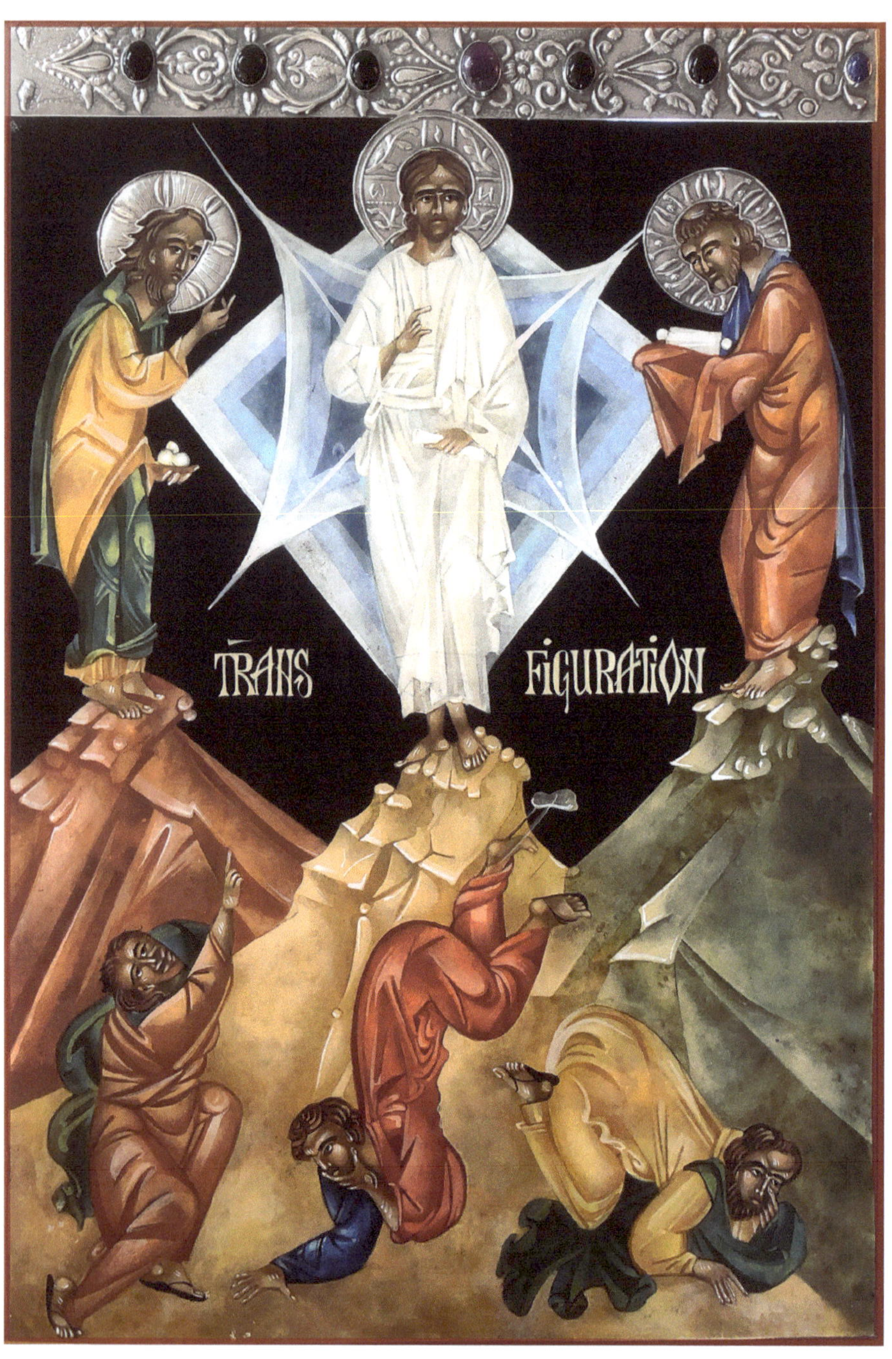

TRANS FIGURATION

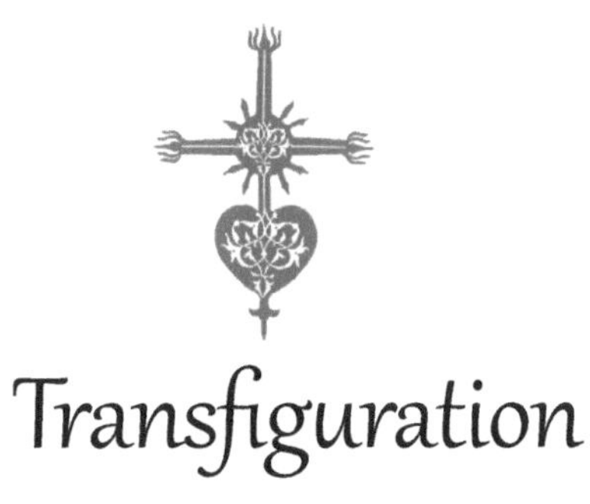

Transfiguration

FOR THE DISCIPLES TO FATHOM THE TEACHING, "I AM THAT
I AM", THEY WILL HAVE TO UNCOVER THEIR FACES, UNSTOP
THEIR EARS, AND STAND TO SPEAK WITH GOD

We find the Transfiguration story in the three Synoptic Gospels. Jesus is accompanied by three disciples from His "inner circle," Peter, James, and John. Jesus invites them to ascend Mount Tabor. On this mountain, the disciples are amazed to recognize Jesus "transfigured" before their eyes. He becomes transparent and ethereal; he now stands outside the constraints of time and space.

This is the first time we see Christ in his transcendent nature where the sensible and intelligible are one. He is the incarnate unseen spirit reflected in three dimensions: body, mind, and soul. Christ is the fulfillment of the Messianic expectations of the Old Testament. The three figures at the top stand in another dimension. Christ is speaking with dead people. Elijah the prophet is on the left, standing on Mt Carmel—lifted to heaven in his fiery chariot. Moses is on the right, standing on Sinai—holding the Torah, the first five books of the Hebrew scriptures, the Teachings. Four icons: Death of Mother Mary, Jesus' Ascension, Descent into Hades, and this one, The Transfiguration, all include a mandorla, signifying divine action taking place in sacred space, to emphasize transformation. The four events are theophanies, situations that cannot be fully explained with words but only experienced.

The accompanying disciples are on the ground: James, left, covering his face after falling backward; John, covering his eyes, shown falling head-over-heels with a dislodged sandal; and Peter, on the right, just beginning to rise to speak.

Who wouldn't want to be transformed by God? The three disciples falling away with fear at the bottom use their hands to hear no evil, see no evil, and speak no evil in gestures of avoidance. For the disciples to fathom the teaching, "I am that I am", they must uncover their faces, unstop their ears, and stand to speak with God directly.

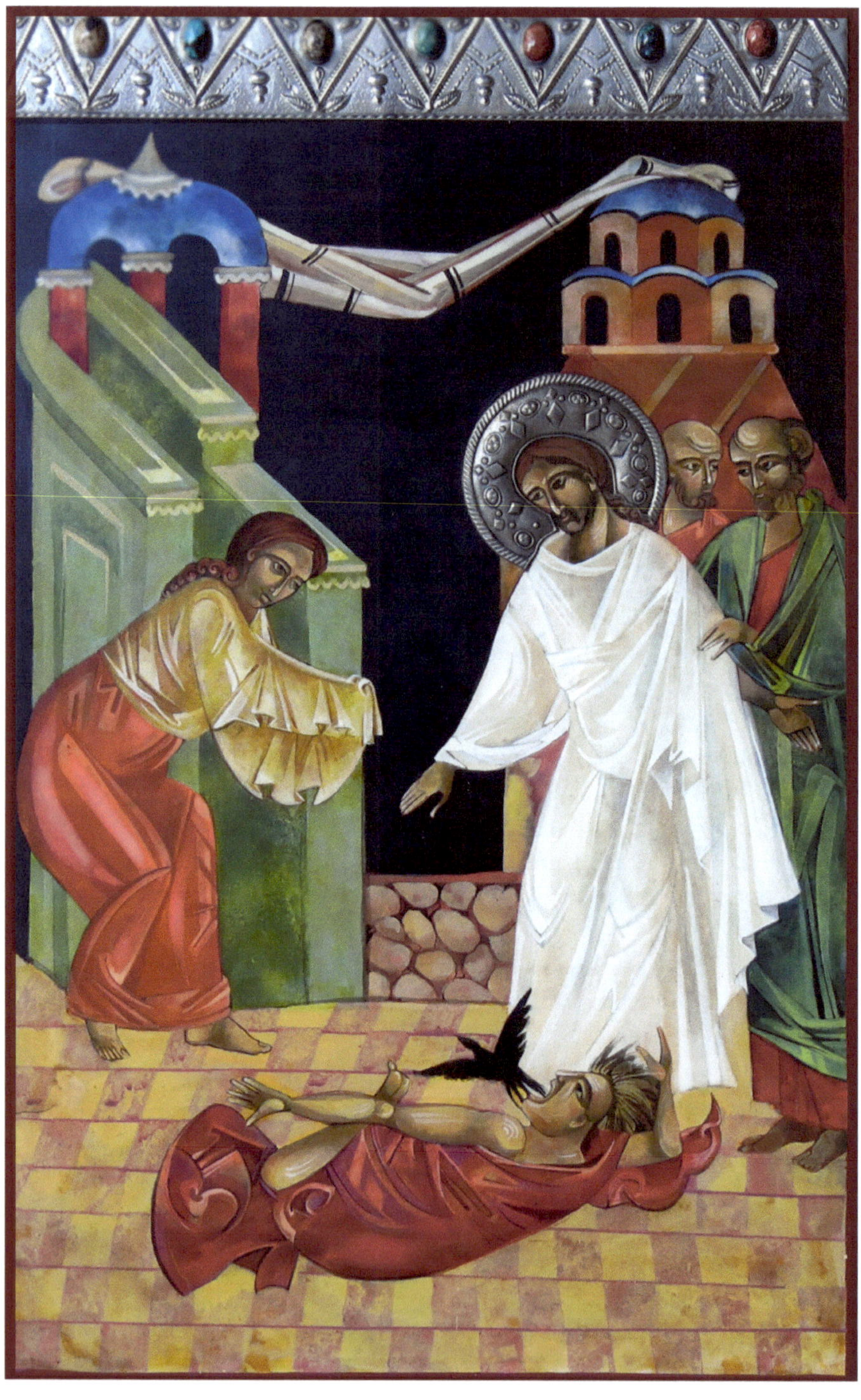

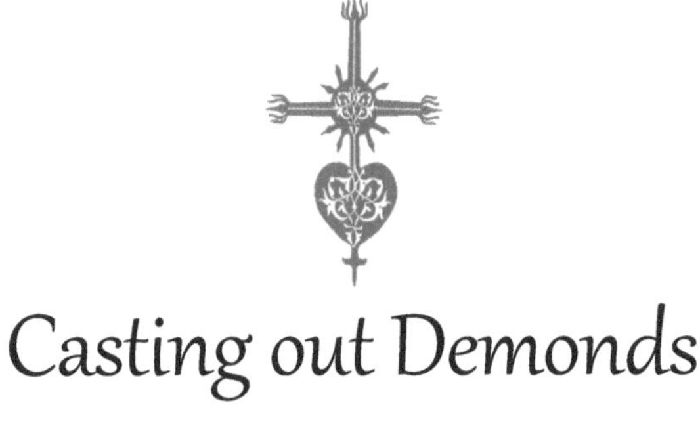

Casting out Demonds

SHE ARRIVES OVERWHELMED WITH GRATITUDE FOR CURING HER FRIEND AND RECOGNIZES ALL THINGS ARE POSSIBLE.

Jesus' third healing is told in John's Gospel 5:1-15. The healing accounts are glimpses into the power and glory of the divine, foretold in the Old Testament scriptures. Jesus turns water into wine at a wedding in Cana, casts out demons, raises Lazarus from the dead, and here heals a cripple at the Pool of Bethesda; each represents radical change. Icons of signs and wonders that illustrate God's plan for abundant life in our world.

The life of Jesus the man, hammers home the human potential for Christ's healing, wholeness, and all manner of extraordinary phenomenon, made vividly present for those who have ears to hear and eyes to see.

Excavations have uncovered a 2nd century BC sanctuary and pool and a separate water source, the Pool of Siloam, mentioned in the Gospel of John. The text tells us that the water was "stirred up" daily. People believed it was from an angel or super-natural action. They believed the water healed the first person to enter each day. At this point in history, illnesses, and disabilities were considered punishment for a person's sins. In this icon, the lame person is holding onto wooden "walkers", a version of "crutches" for paraplegics.

The Jewish theologian stands with those who are ill, one with his head wrapped up tight in a prayer shawl. It displeases him that Jesus cured the lame man by telling him to pick up his mat and walk. They accuse Jesus of unlawful healing, saying you cannot be "working" on the Sabbath. Jesus defends himself, referencing God as "My Father" which angered the Jewish authorities even more. Calling God His father was sacrilegious.

Throughout the icon series, people being bound by cloth on their heads or around their legs is intentional, to highlight the human condition of being bound up by our beliefs. The story of Jesus can teach us to reflect on where reality and the mystery of God intersect.

POOL BATHESDA

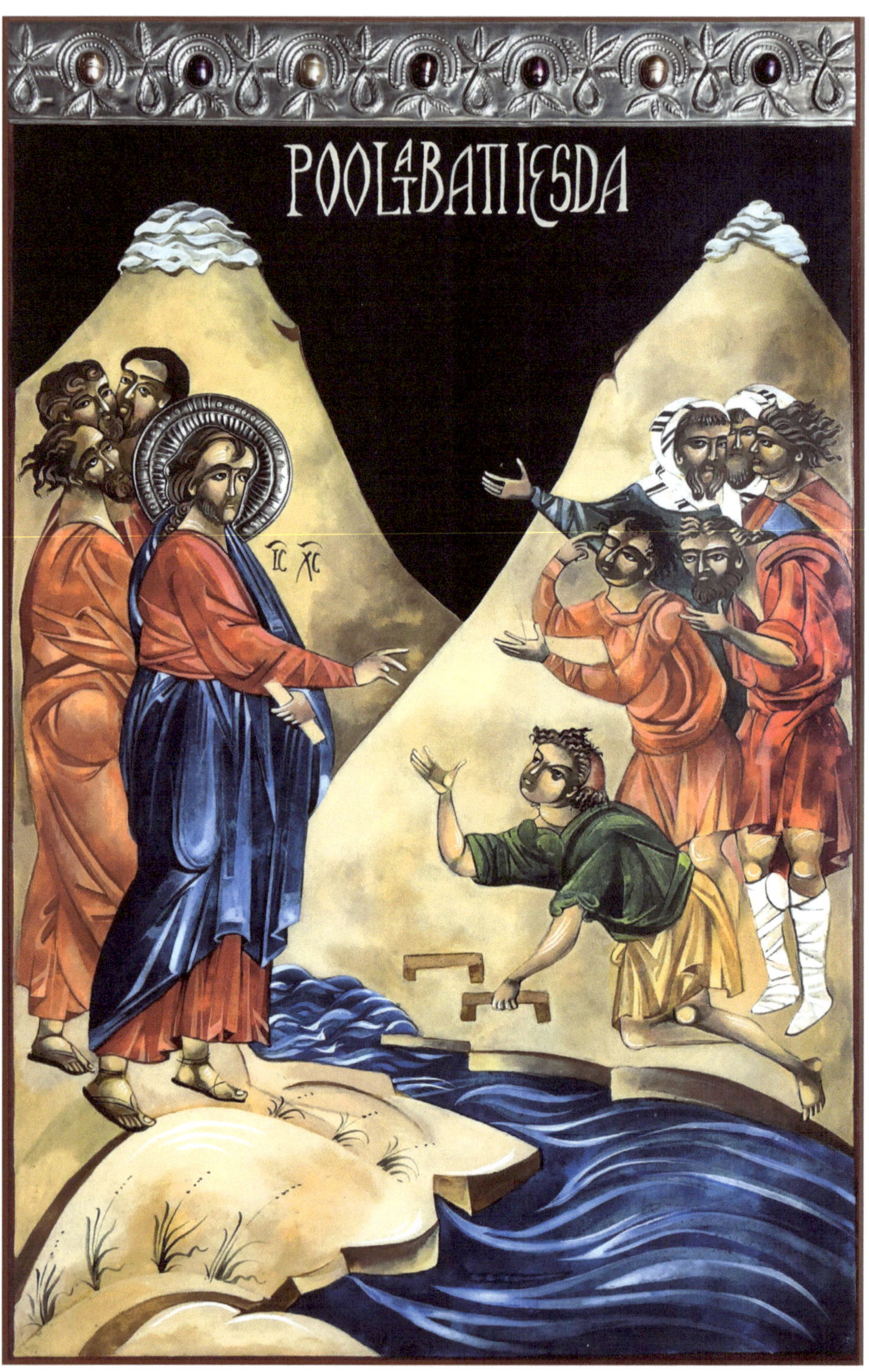

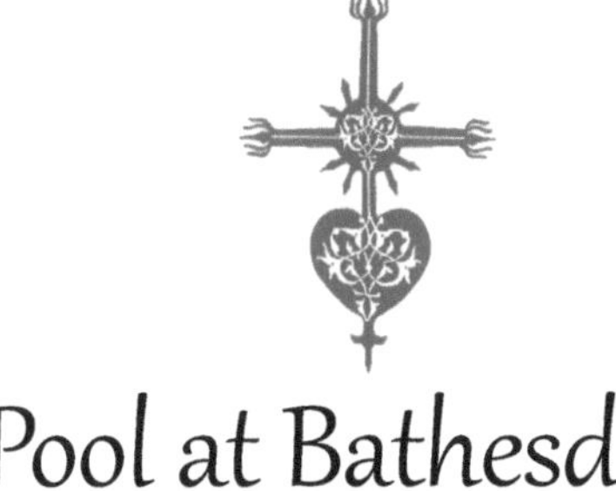

Pool at Bathesda

Jesus' third healing, when he heals a lame man is told in John's Gospel 5:1-15. The healing accounts are glimpses into the power and glory of the divine, foretold in the Old Testament scriptures. Jesus turns water into wine at a wedding in Cana, casts out demons, raises Lazarus from the dead, and here heals a cripple at the Pool of Bethesda; each represents radical change.

I have often wondered where the line is between God and the unrestricted life of Christ in us. The life of Jesus hammers home the human potential for healing, wholeness, and all manner of extraordinary phenomenon, made vividly present for those who have ears to hear and eyes to see.

The text tells us that the water was "stirred up" daily. People believed it was from an angel or supernatural action. They believed the water healed the first person to enter each day. At this point in history, illnesses and disabilities were considered punishment for a person's sins. In this icon, the lame person is holding onto wooden "walkers", a version of "crutches" for paraplegics.

The Jewish theologian stands with those who are ill, one with his head wrapped up tight in a prayer shawl. It displeases him that Jesus cured the lame man by telling him to pick up his mat and walk. They accuse Jesus of unlawful healing, saying you cannot be "working" on the Sabbath. Jesus defends himself, referencing God as "My Father" which angered the Jewish authorities even more. Calling God His father was sacrilegious.

Throughout the icon series, people being bound by cloth on their heads or around their legs is intentional, to highlight the human condition of being bound up by our beliefs. The story of Jesus can teach us to re-frame where reality and the mystery of God intersect. One more recurring visual feature in narrative iconography is the color of Jesus' garments. The colors are most often blue and red. The red of his interior clothing signifies his earthly nature, while the blue outer garment is symbolic of his cosmic nature. Jesus is a manifestation of God's energy, which is infinite, like the cosmos.

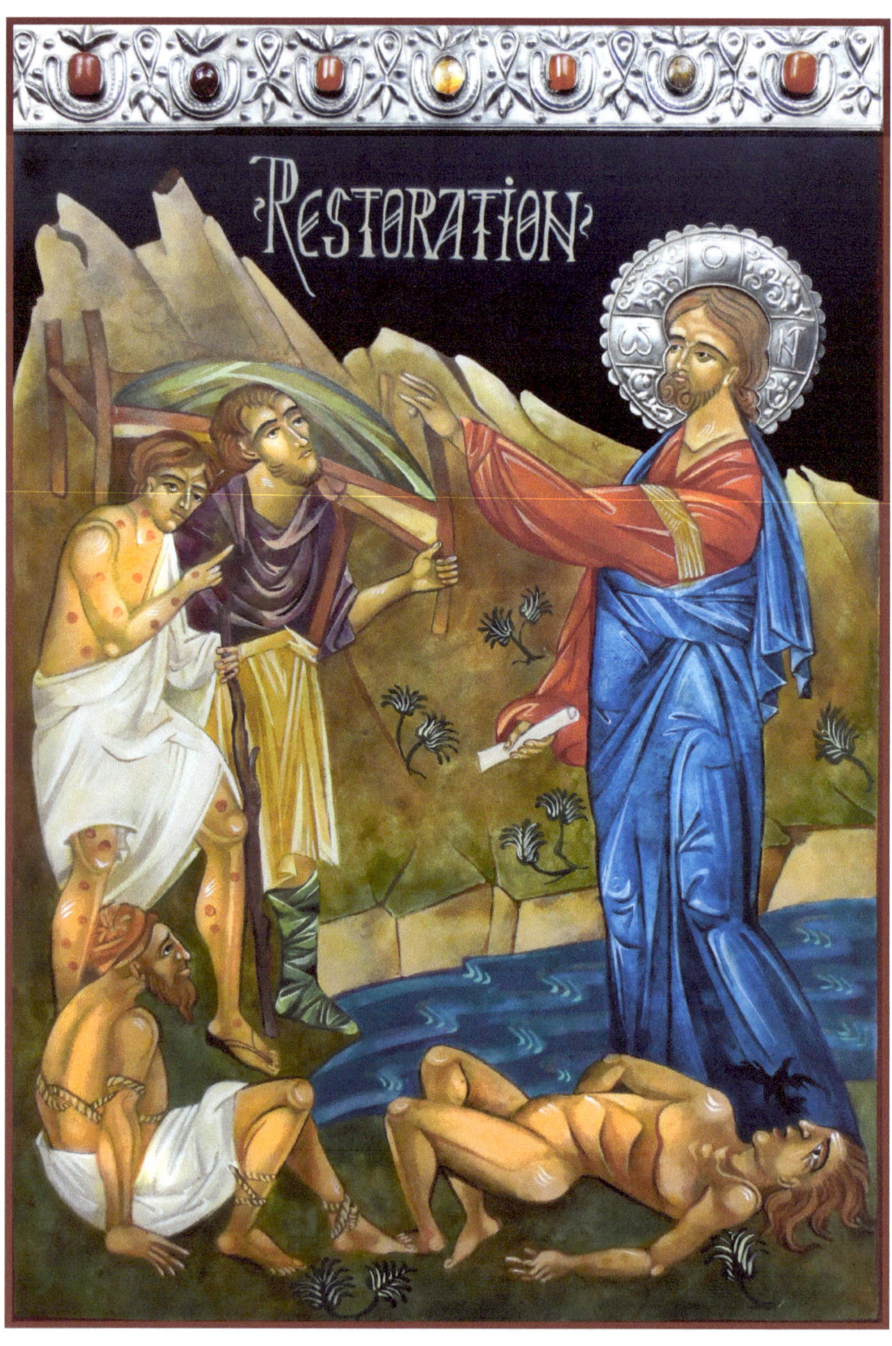
Restoration

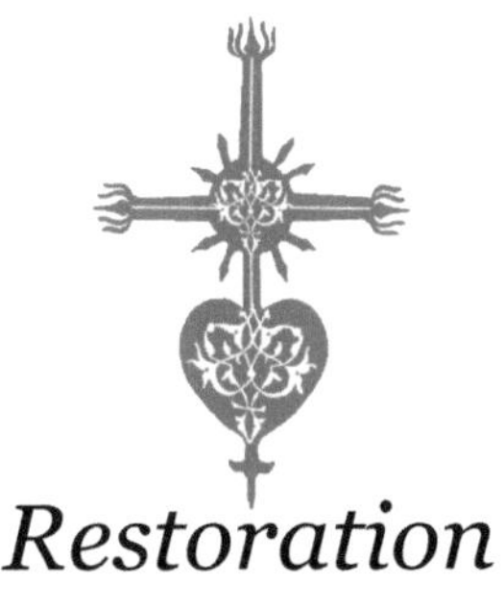

Restoration

The contorted body is troubling; the agony is familiar to those who feel the unnamed woman is distressed, out of control, or unable to speak.

One of the disciples reaches forward, touching Jesus on the arm as if calling him back and away from this strange encounter, they are cautious. From a biblical perspective, demons are depicted as malevolent beings who oppose God and seek to bring harm, temptation, and confusion to humanity. These spiritual entities are believed to possess a certain level of intelligence, influence, and power.

Another woman approaches with covered hands, seeing this man approach with compassion and fearlessness. Her covered hands show her reverence for sanctity; perhaps she needs healing herself. She arrives, overwhelmed with gratitude for curing her friend, and recognizes all things are possible.
Iconographers use a technique to distinguish the difference between generated light of the sun and the interior spiritual light of God. Divine light does not cast shadows, it comes from within, shining life-giving glory onto everything it encounters. The garments seem to sparkle or appear to be fractured with abstract design. Buildings are not meant to identify or document a specific place or historical city. Receding vanishing point perspective and abstract forms become design elements to convey the event took place in an actual structure or city scape.

Events happening in narrative icons can happen anywhere. The flatness of the walls, draped clothes, or the shape of the domed buildings all help to abstract the composition, distorting reality to emphasize the activity taking place in a spiritual dimension. Black areas in an icon are usually small and mark the absence of God.

All these visual features push the limits of realism, taking the viewer out of this earthly world. These techniques serve to draw us into the sacramental scene out beyond what we are witnessing

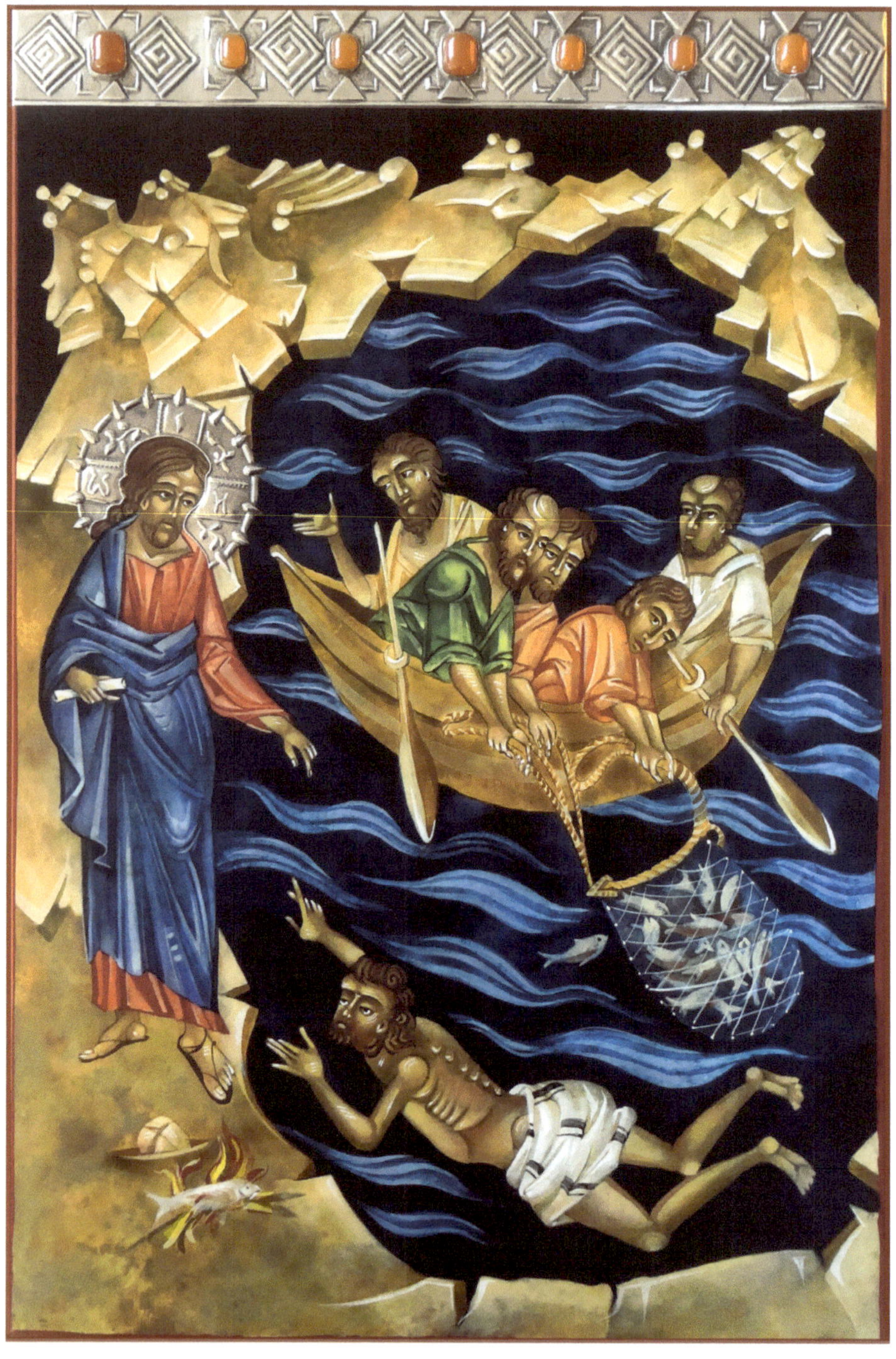

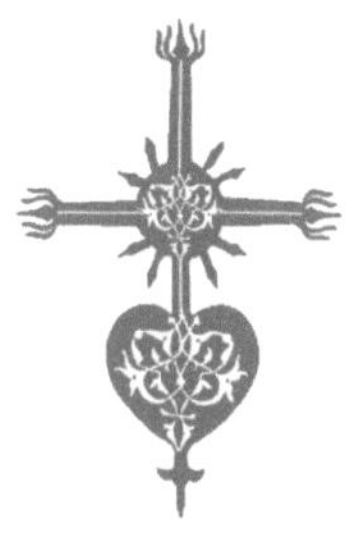

Walking on Water

The gospels of Matthew, Mark, and John, all record Peter and Jesus walking on the water. Peter asked. "If it is you, tell me to come to you on the water." He acknowledges Jesus has bent the law of nature and calls to him before the other disciples. He wants to walk or go to Jesus regardless of the distance or the fact Jesus is standing on the water.

In the story, Jesus commands Peter to "come" to Him on the water. Peter took one step in faith to get out of the boat and onto the water. Peter did not experience the supernatural power of God that allowed him to walk on water until he trusted in what he saw as something impossible.

Distracted by fear and the thinking mind, Peter lost his trust in what was happening and reverted back to what he could understand. We become less when we cleave to the limits of our physical world as if it is the only reality. With just a little faith, we are capable of greater wisdom, love, trust, and mystery, and open ourselves to every potential for God's unscientific presence. It is easy to lose our determined focus on Jesus and become consumed with concerns for our outside world.

Peter looked away from Jesus, his faith was lost and he sank. When we keep our eyes on spirit, the limits and confinement of this reality will disappear. Our life can be a tumultuous storm, but the spiritual dimension is always there for guidance. Imagine Peter leaving the boat on his own, to swim in a storm.

He is successful in this "impossible situation." It's a comical story where two dimensions collide. We can stay in the boat for security, instead of venturing out on the waters of faith where we fear we might drown. It is difficult to reject the safe and familiar and choose to walk, led by faith, through a tempest.

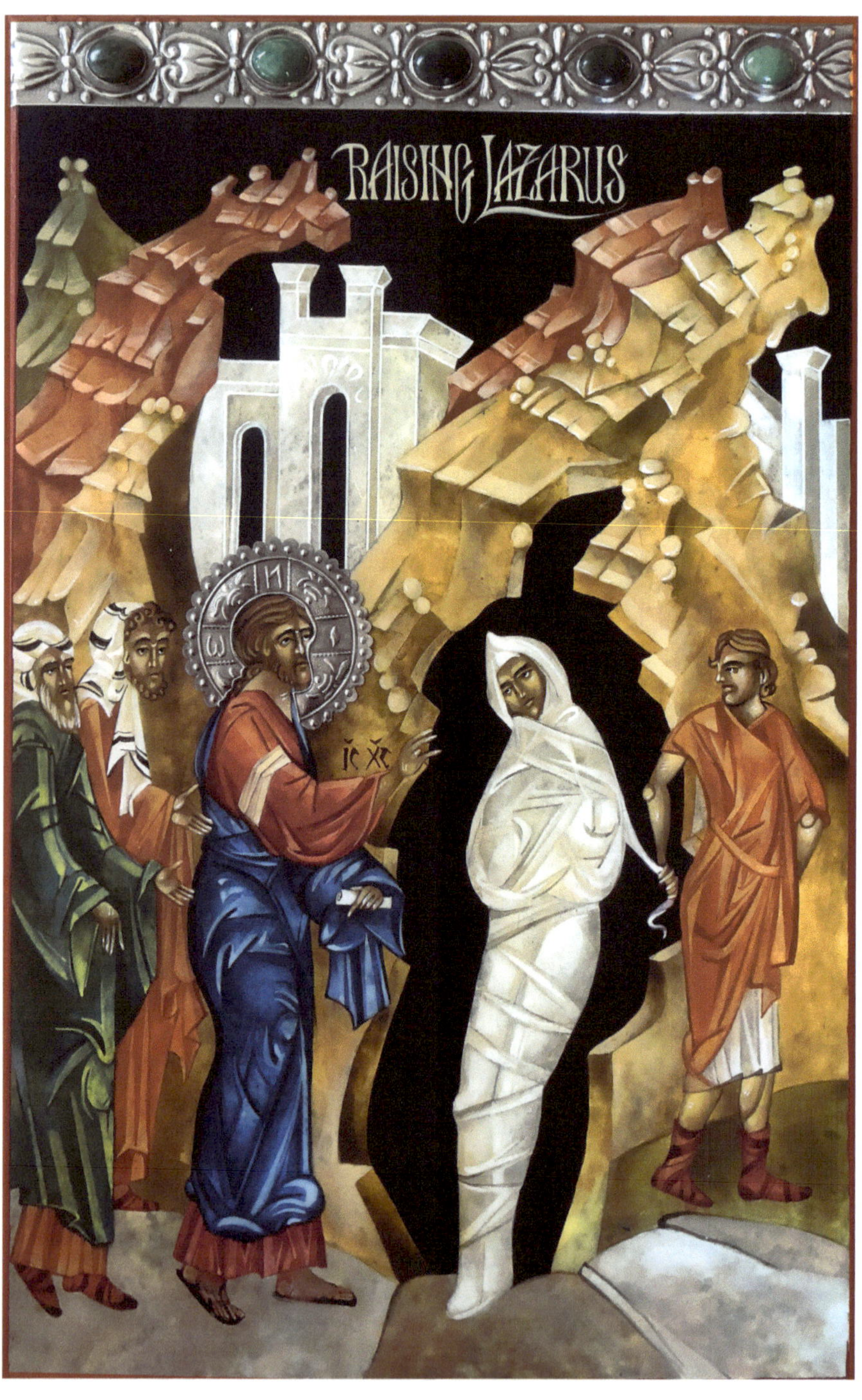

RAISING LAZARUS
ĪC ХC

Raising Lazarus

Jesus, the Word, reveals himself to the world and to those who know him. We are told that Jesus weeps for his dear friend, Lazarus. He brings his friend back from the dead with a wave of his hand, using divine authority. He says, "Rise and step into the light." as a direct command. The event frames the seventh miracle. Signs of God's glory are seven intercessions where Jesus bends reality to illustrate the power of the Christ in Him to his followers. It is clever foreshadowing set up in the Bible to illustrate Jesus's resurrection from the tomb.

We see the omnipresent scroll in Jesus' hand — an element throughout iconography that amplifies the idea that Jesus is the fulfillment of Old Testament prophecies. Ezekiel 37:14 says: "And you shall know that I am the LORD, when I open your graves and bring you up from your tombs... I will put My Spirit in you, and you will live, and I will settle you in your land."

The transformation from death into life is a riddle and is happening outside the walled city. Jesus and Ezekiel both know about dry dead bones. They know who puts the spirit in us. Death is not an end place of confinement, but rather a thin veil of transition. Lazarus, on the right, is emerging from his tomb, wrapped in white bands of cloth like a mummy. Sisters Mary and Martha are bowing down at Jesus' feet in gratitude. The disciples are standing behind Jesus. A man is there to "un- bind" Lazarus while turning away from the smell. The Bible says the body already smelled of decay.

Traditional prayer shawls bind their heads as they wait to see this situation unfold in disbelief and awe. Notice the stylized mountains stretching towards the heavens. If we follow the cave or tomb behind Lazarus, both mountain peaks stretch towards the heavens, bearing generations of small stones upon their slopes. An ancient Jewish tradition is to place stones atop the graves of the departed to commemorate the person and note they have been visited. These stones are symbolic of eternity and the continuity of life.

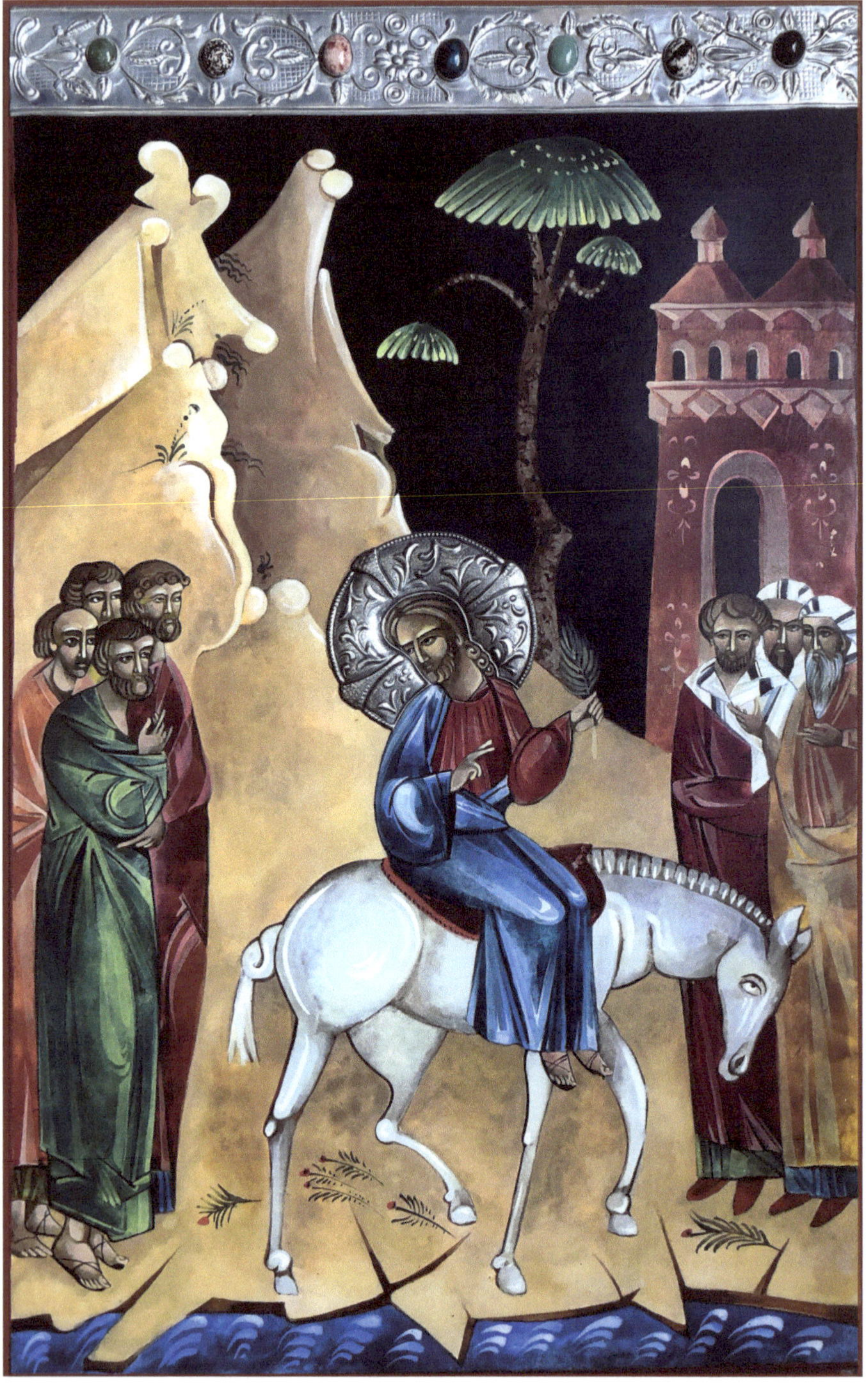

Entry into Jerusalem

Jesus' triumphal entry into the city of Jerusalem riding a donkey happens the week before Passover and his Crucifixion. Jesus looks back over his shoulders to console his followers as they grumble their concern for his return to Jerusalem. He has no fear as he approaches the city where he will be betrayed, abandoned, and murdered. It is interesting to me, how early iconographers worked out a way of describing followers and those who cast doubt and judgement on Jesus the teacher.

This story opens the first scene in the passion narrative that leads up to his Crucifixion. Matthew and Luke mention the people spreading out their cloaks on the roadway before Jesus. In other icons you would see children in the palm trees cutting down the branches, an ancient symbol of victory.

The earliest iconography of Jesus entering Jerusalem show the donkey floating off the ground. In more contemporary icons, the donkey is positioned realistically, walking on the ground. Yet in doing so, the original message loses an important theological tenant. The ancient master iconographers used the floating donkey as another indication showing how Jesus changes the spiritual dimension of what we expect. Many saints around the world have been reported as having levitated; they rise or float as if to defy the weight or burden of their earthly body.

We see Jesus traveling from the Mount of Olives on the left, toward the Holy City, on the right. On the mountain slope we see a dark shapes. There are many small dark or black spaces in icons, some are windows on buildings, and some indicate the caves where hermits and mystics might have lived.

A building or cave is a metaphor for the hermit's life, they maintain an interior conversation with God as they seek his wisdom and light. Black is the color to represent the absence of God where we work to live in the light. Many sages have chosen to renounce the world and live in extreme denial of the physical to attain the heights of what it means to be spiritual. The dark night of the soul is a term used by mystics to describe the absence of being able to relate to the world as we know it. Without their commitment to test and be tested by the limits of what we accept as reality, all of creation would remain in darkness.

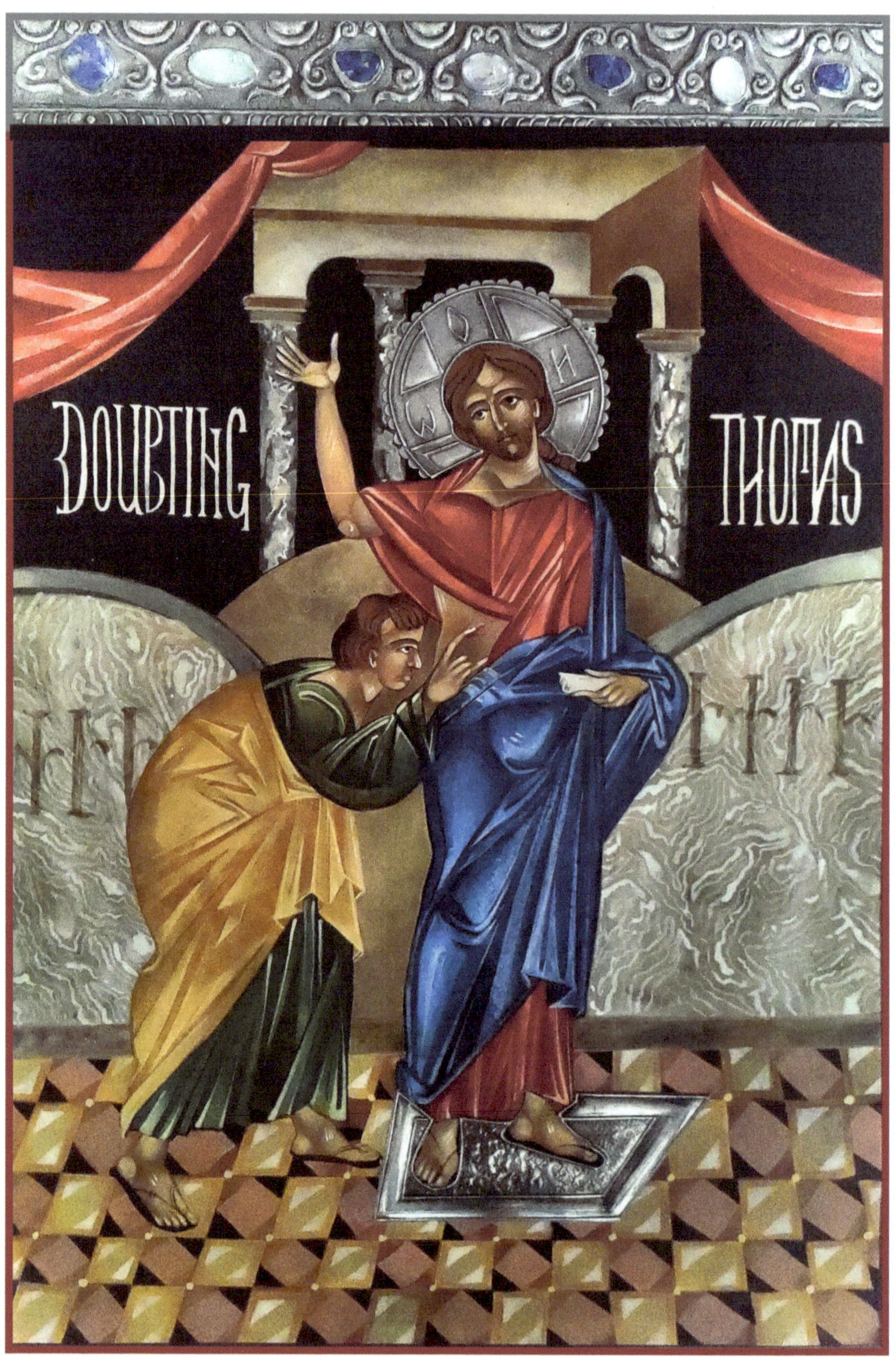

DOUBTING THOMAS

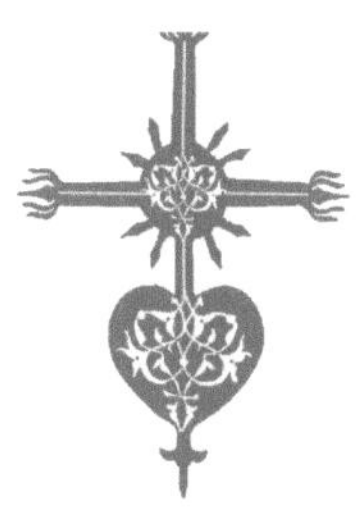

Doubting Thomas

Only John's gospel has this story, 20th chapter of John. The original icon, done by the Russian Novgorod School of Iconography, shows a red gash in Christs' side with Thomas' finger reaching into it. Thomas is curious to reach into the wound, to get proof for what others have been saying, that their teacher is NOT dead.

We learn that the disciples had gathered behind closed doors out of fear of the Jewish authorities. The red cloth draped over the wall and building is the iconic symbol for a scene taking place inside. He is haloed and robed in his traditional red tunic and blue cloak holding a white scroll. Jesus, eight days after his death, is able to enter the room and here we see his intimate encounter with Thomas.

Thomas actually took Jesus up on his offer to reach out and put your hand here and touch his wound. John's Gospel tells us that at this point, Thomas proclaims, "My Lord and My God!" He has realized that when one looks upon the face of Jesus, he is looking upon perfected humanity, we are told Thomas is the first person to know this.

This particular icon's story is for anyone who had doubted the reality of a divine spirit unseen. Christ has always been present in my life, everywhere and sometimes just beneath a thin garment waiting for me to reach out and touch him. Sacred space, spiritual awe, divine understanding, and mystical awareness cannot be limited to any one place or even in any one religion. If we believe with our whole heart, mind, and soul that God is everywhere, the question becomes where can there be no God?

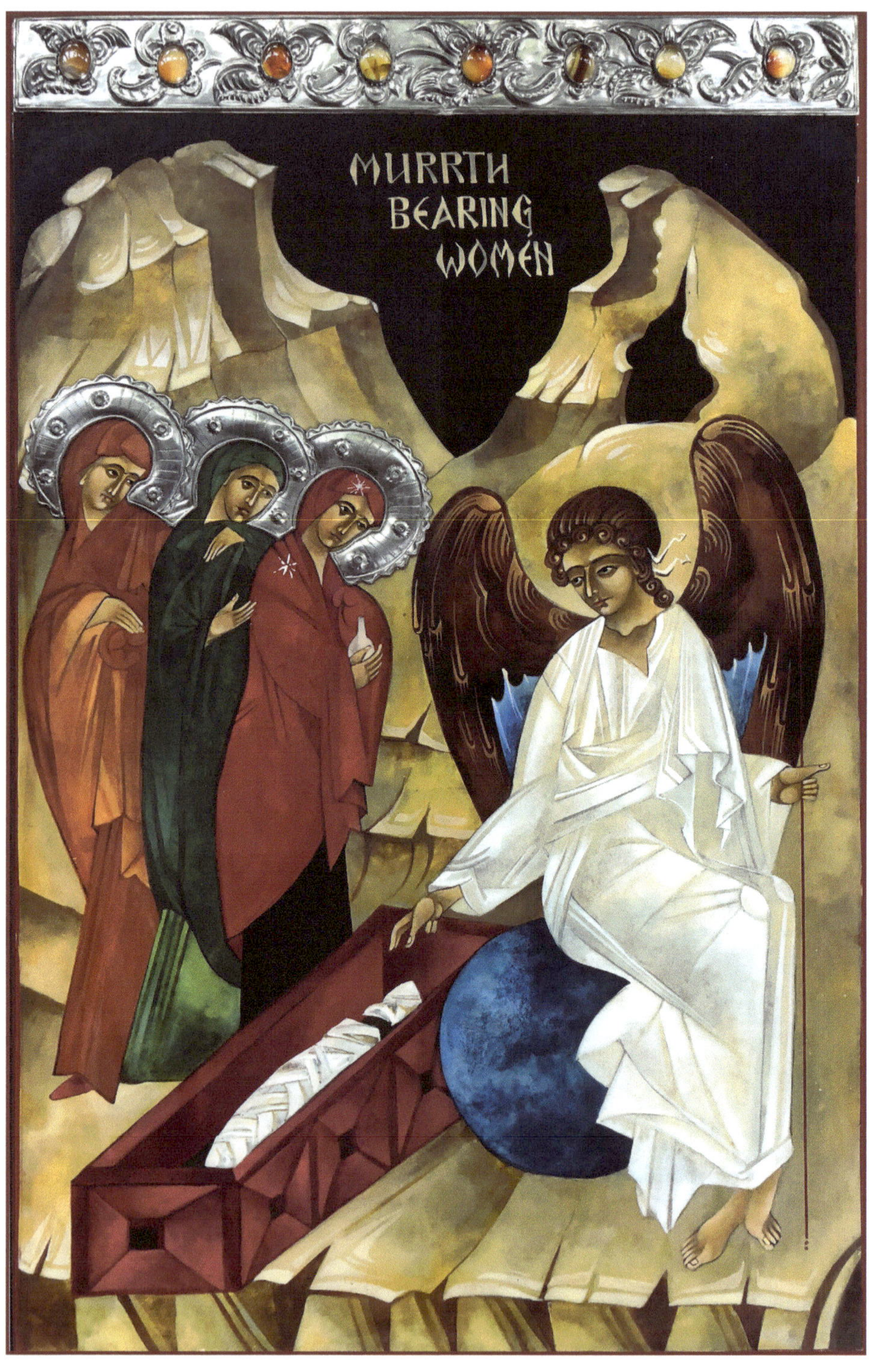

MURRTH
BEARING
WOMEN

Women who go to the Tomb

We know the women stayed throughout Jesus's passion and came to the tomb to anoint his dead body. The three figures, from left to right, includes three women, Mary, Suzanne and the other Mary. Matthew 27:62-28:15

After the Sabbath, at dawn on the first day of the week, Mary Magdalene and the other Mary went to look at the tomb." (not to be confused with Mary the mother of Jesus, she is not named after the resurrection) There was a violent earthquake, for an angel of the Lord came down from heaven and, going to the tomb, rolled back the stone and sat on it. His appearance was like lightning, and his clothes were white as snow.

The angel said to the women, "Do not be afraid, for I know that you are looking for Jesus, who was crucified. He is not here; he has risen, just as he said. Come and see the place where he lay. Then go quickly and tell his disciples: This clearly states Jesus had sent more than one woman to the disciples with the message of the resurrection.

The binding up of a body, wrapping it in a swaddling cloth or entombed within a shroud is a curious tradition. All through the collection, you find examples of being bound; the birth of Mary and the birth of Jesus, Lazarus, the Dormition of Mary, the various feet and heads of those who witness these events, among others. We are called to assist one another and unbind the bound up.

The Egyptians and Peruvians wrapped the bodies of the dead as if to protect them or perhaps to detain their freedom in leaving us. Isaiah bound his son, Jacob, and Mary's soul is bound at her death. It is worth reflecting on the idea of binding one another or binding ourselves. Matthew 16:19 says, "whatever you bind on earth will be bound in heaven, and whatever you loose on earth will be loosed in heaven."

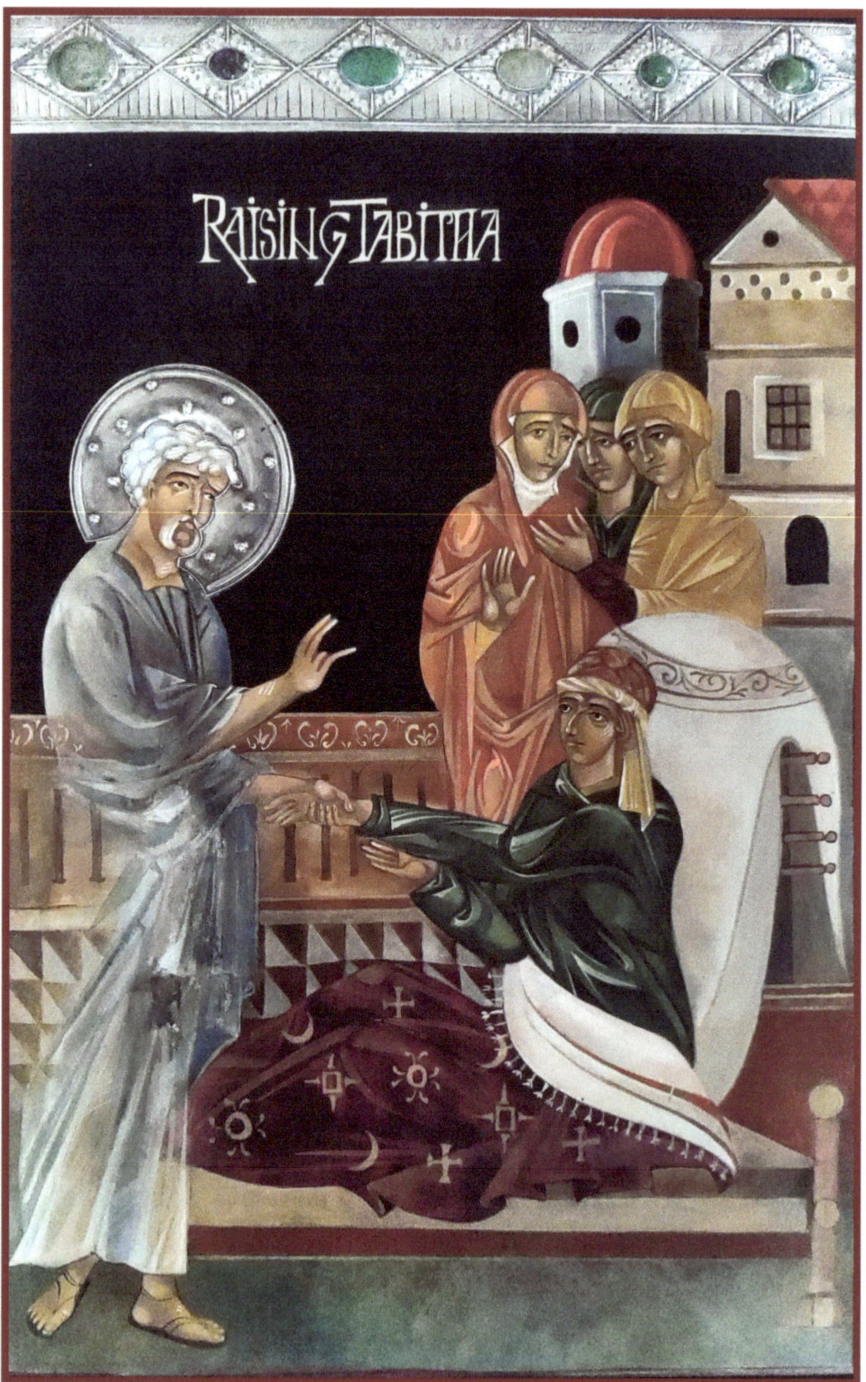
RAISING TABITHA

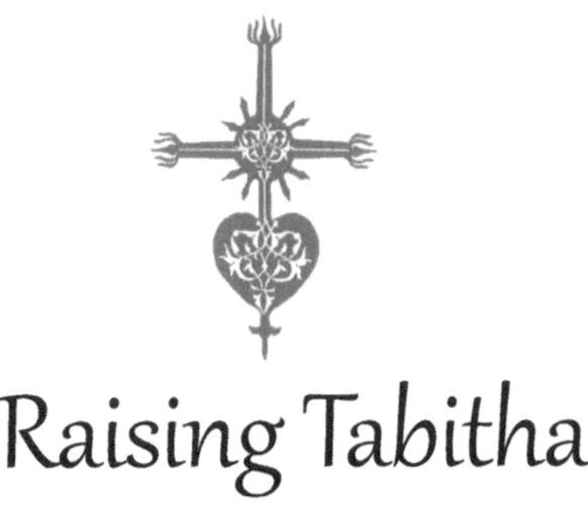

Raising Tabitha

The Orthodox use narrative icons to reveal that the man named is the flawless, blameless, and perfected image of God. In Colossians 1:15, Paul claims, "He is the image of the invisible God." One of the greatest mysteries of the entire story is how does humanity comprehend an invisible God? Christians have built their theology around the idea that Jesus is the only man to achieve this ranking. Jesus became the visible word of God, a human being who walked among us. Yet in my mind. the Christ essence that was housed in Jesus the man becomes visible through all of humanity as we bring to life acts of love and compassion, the way Peter raises Tabitha in this next icon. It is the energy of Christ that changes humanity.

Everyone in the city of Joppa loved Tabitha. She was always doing good, helping the poor, and making garments for others. One day Tabitha grew sick and died. Women washed her body, then placed it in an upstairs room. They sent for the apostle Peter, who was nearby in Lydda. Clearing everyone from the room, Peter fell to his knees and prayed. He said to her, "Tabitha, arise." Sitting upright, Peter presented her to her friends alive. Acts 9:36-42. Peter uses the power of Christ within. When Jesus ate and drank with a flesh and bone body, he was not bound by the laws of the physical realm. Jesus is the first example of a spirit-man not hindered by any physical existence. We have been promised that when we walk in divine light, we too shall be as He is.

In the encounter between doubting Thomas and the Risen Jesus, John 20:19–28, we see Thomas's need to be affirmed. Believing that someone could be fatally wounded and resurrected at the same time is a conundrum. This might be the primary pastoral message of the Gospel; we are affirmed when we examine the life of Jesus and his behavior, modeling ourselves after his example. Jesus walked with us in the world, contained in a body of flesh and blood and inseparable from spirit. It is the spirit within Peter who raises Tabitha, he has been changed by the spirit of Christ within and given the power to raise the dead.

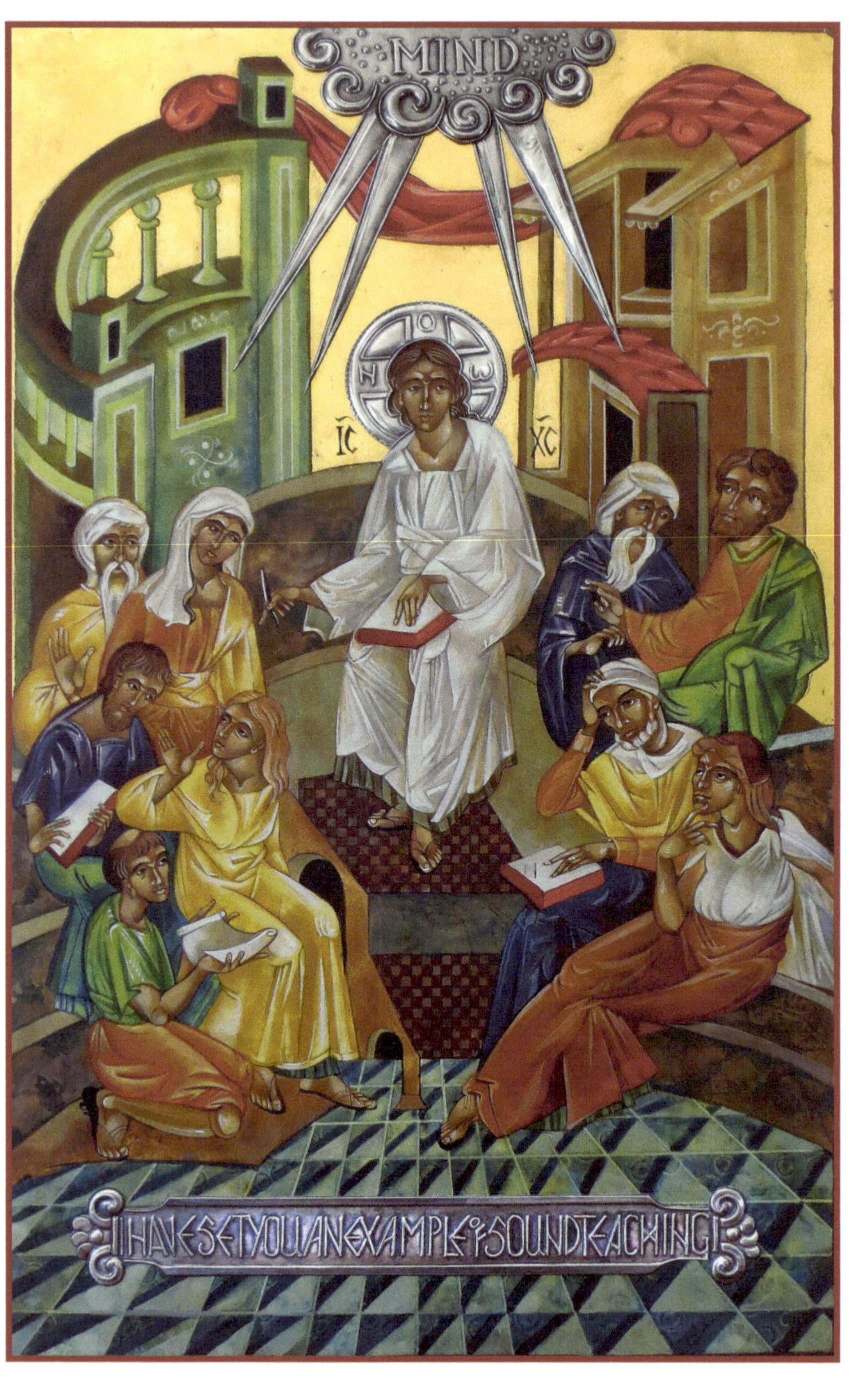

MIND
IC XC
I HAVE SET YOU AN EXAMPLE OF SOUND TEACHING

Entry into Jerusalem

Jesus' triumphal entry into the city of Jerusalem riding a donkey happens the week before Passover and his Crucifixion Jesus looks back over his shoulders to console his followers as they grumble their concern for his return to Jerusalem. He has no fear as he approaches the city where he will be betrayed, abandoned, and murdered. Jesus' purpose in riding into Jerusalem was to make public His claim to be their Messiah and King of Israel in fulfillment of Old Testament prophecy, hence the scroll in his hand.

This story opens the first scene in the passion narrative that leads up to his crucifixion. Matthew and Luke mention the people spreading out their cloaks on the roadway before Jesus. We see the children in the palm trees cutting down the branches. The palms mentioned in John's gospel are ancient symbols of victory. There were many who, though they did not believe in Christ as Savior, nevertheless hoped that perhaps He would be to them a great temporal deliverer. These are the ones who hailed Him as King with their many hosannas, recognizing Him as the Son of David who came in the name of the Lord. We will come to see, His is not a kingdom of armies and splendor but of lowliness and servanthood.

We see Jesus traveling from the Mount of Olives on the left, toward the Holy City, on the right. John's gospel, written sixty years after the event, gives some of the most interesting details, including the fact that the night before the triumphal entry, Jesus had an intimate supper in the home of Lazarus, Martha, and Mary, as recorded in John 12:1-11.

A building or cave is a metaphor for the hermit's life, they maintain an interior conversation with God as they seek his wisdom and light. Black is the color to represent the absence of God where we work to live in the light. Many sages have chosen to renounce the world and live in extreme denial of the physical to attain the heights of what it means to be spiritual. The dark night of the soul is a term used by mystics to describe the absence of being able to relate to the world as we know it. Without their commitment to test and be tested by the limits of what we accept as reality, all of creation would remain in darkness.

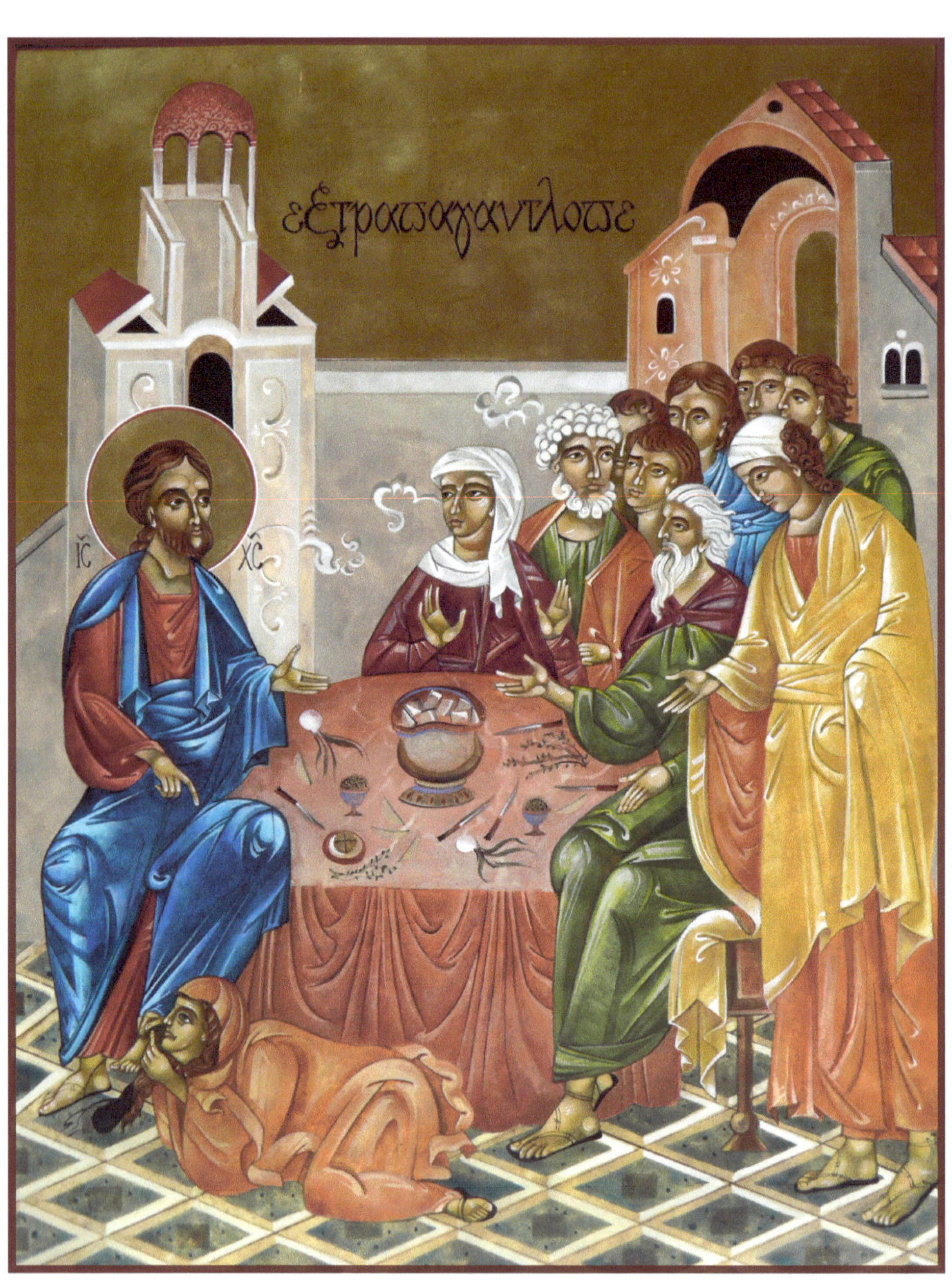

ΙϹ ΧϹ

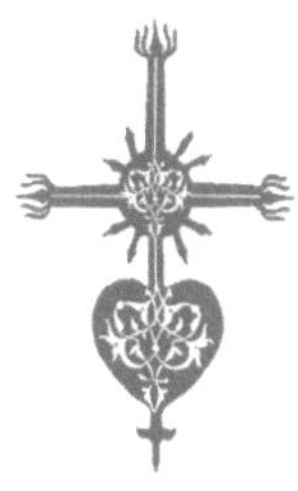

Extravagant Love

All four Gospel writers include versions of Jesus' anointing by a woman. Luke 7:36-50: "At the home of a Pharisee, a weeping, sinful woman anoints Jesus' feet with expensive ointment and her tears, drying them with her hair. Matthew 26:6–13 and Mark 14:3–9 recall the event occurred in the house of Simon the Leper in Bethany. John 12:5-6 it states the disciples were at the house of Lazarus in Bethany. It is not clear from the text where the event took place or who the woman is. We miss the message if we get stuck on the sinful woman in a house with the disciples bickering and not the act of forgiveness. The story is the portrayal of one woman's selfless gesture of love for Jesus. Might we not do better to focus on themes of forgiveness, generosity, and courage illustrated in the story?

The witnessing disciples complain about the wasteful gesture of devotion, saying the money could have been better spent on the poor, Judus say- ing, "Why wasn't this perfume sold and the money given to the poor? It was worth a year's wages." Judas did not say this because he cared about the poor, but because he was a thief; as keeper of the money bag, he used to help himself to what was put into it.

Not one account names Mary Magdalene as this woman. It was Augustine, writing in the 4th century, who decided this was a story of Mary of Mag- dalene. Because the weeping woman in Luke's account was a "sinner," Au- gustine proclaimed, this woman, Mary Magdalene, was a prostitute. There is no Biblical evidence for this accusation, but the tarnished reputation has regretfully stuck to Mary Magdalene for centuries. I have her standing, present at the encounter, and slightly larger than the others.

Regardless of who the woman is, the scene portrays a noisy crowd of priests and disciples who strongly object to this woman. The men discuss Jesus' time coming to a close; in contrast, this woman wants only to express her devotion and humility. Yet, her understated action demonstrates power in perseverance. The woman low-ers her entire self to the floor before Jesus to steal one intimate moment with the one she loves and reveres.

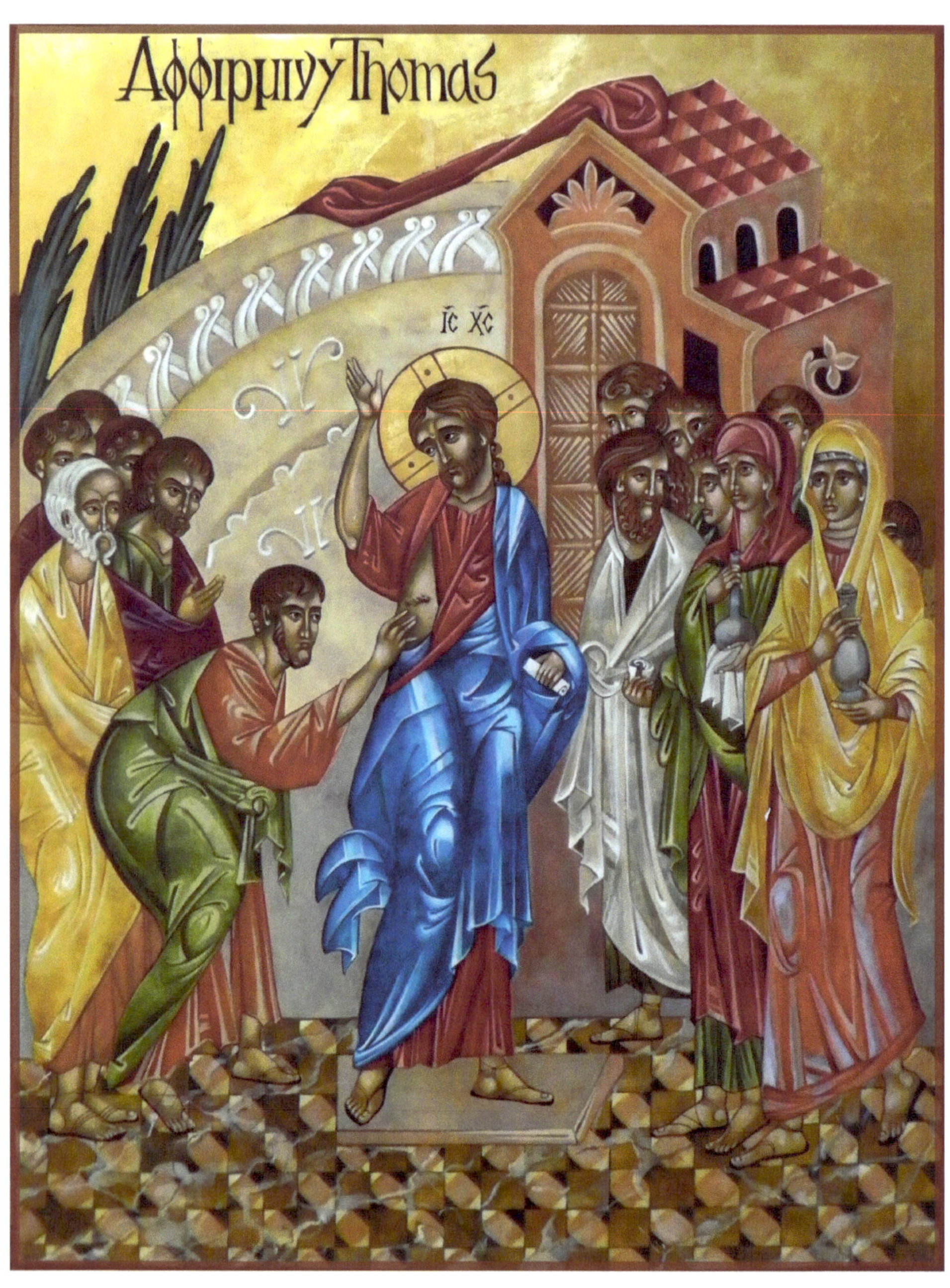

Αψψιρμιγγ Thomas
IC XC

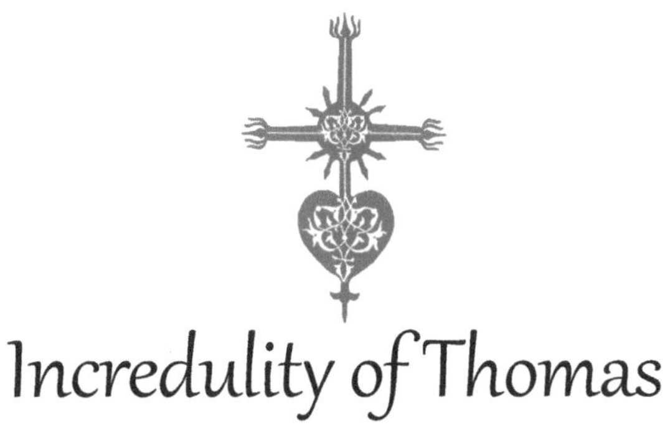

Incredulity of Thomas

The original icon, done by the Russian Novgorod School of Iconography, shows a red gash in Christs' side with Thomas' finger reaching into it. Thomas is curious to reach into the wound. He wants proof and stretches out his finger with courage.

We learn that the disciples had gathered behind closed doors out of fear of the Jewish authorities. This icon shows the closed door behind Thomas. Christ appears eight days after his death and is able to enter the room where the eleven have withdrawn in fear. I have included women in the composition who witness the event, thinking it impossible for Jewish men to leave their wives and children as they hid in the upper room. Trees are waving in the background outside beyond the walls. The red cloth draped over the wall and building is the iconic symbol for a scene taking place inside. He is haloed and robed in his traditional red tunic and blue cloak holding a white scroll.

At this point, I want to share a small reflection. A large part of the collection ended up installed in the St. Thomas Episcopal Church, in Abingdon, Virginia. This was the church where I first heard the voice of God long before my interest in painting icons began.

I was baptized and raised in the Anglican church. At twenty-seven, I had no need for spirituality or church. I went into the church of St. Thomas looking for rest and refuge. Within two hours, I realized I was the source of my own discomfort and needed to find a way to connect to something greater than myself. That day I heard a voice that said, "Be not afraid, I go before you." This particular icon's story is my story. When I painted Christ exposing his side, inviting Thomas to touch him fifteen years later, I was at peace.

The "Doubting Thomas" had become the "Affirming Thomas" and my awareness had shifted between two poles, one of doubt and the other belief. Christ has always been present in my life, everywhere and sometimes just beneath a thin garment waiting for me to reach out and touch him. Sacred space, spiritual awe, divine understanding, and mystical awareness, cannot be limited to any one place. If we believe with our whole heart, mind, and soul that God is everywhere, the question becomes where can there be no God?

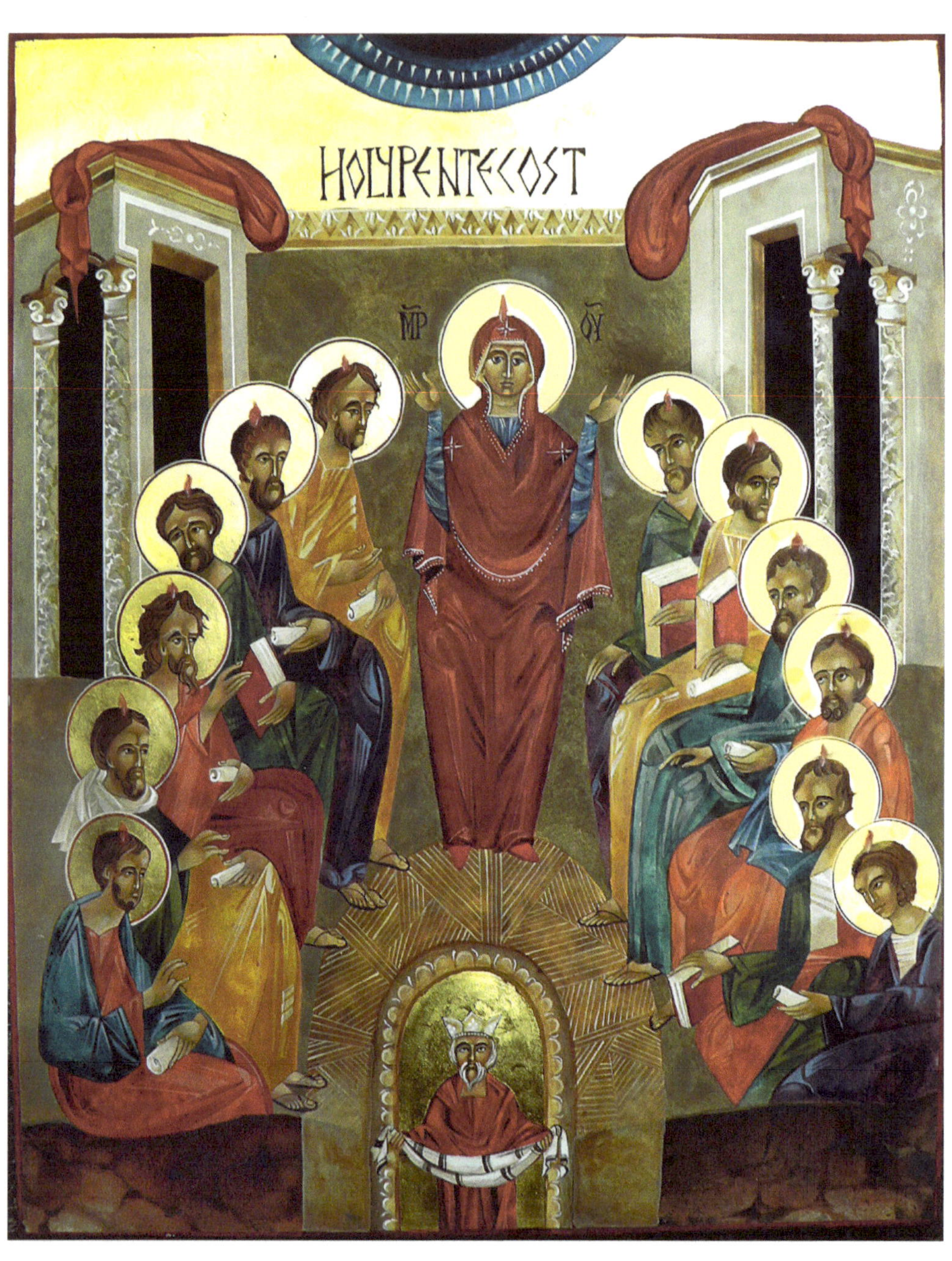

HOLYPENTECOST

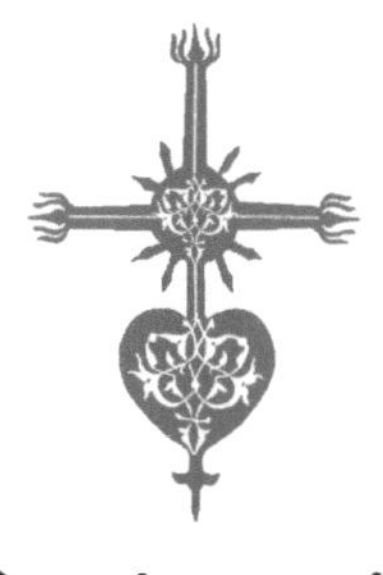

Pentecost

The theology behind what we call Pentecost was framed by the Jewish holiday of Shavuot, or Festival of Weeks, a holiday in honor of the first fruits of the harvest. The annual celebration commemorates receiving the laws of the Torah on Mount Sinai fifty days after the first day of Passover and the Exodus from Egypt. The disciples seated here with Mary are given the fruits of the spirit introduced by Jesus. He is the fulfillment of history giving humanity a new law, to love God with our whole heart, and Love ourselves as we Love each other.

According to the book of Acts, the disciples are gathered in one place. Judas has been replaced with Matthias by casting lots. Four disciples hold books while others hold scrolls. In later icons you find four disciples holding books and are adorned with crosses on their stoles representing how the church hierarchy was forming.

Biblical accounts describe the Holy Spirit as rushing wind and individual tongues of fire descending upon the disciples' heads. In this icon, the Holy Spirit is descending from a heavenly mandorla. The half-circle shaped mandorla is the source of divine wisdom that radiates toward the disciples' heads. Mary presides in the center, she is the chalice that bore the Christ.

Nowhere does the Bible account suggest that Mary, the mother of Jesus, was present. However, the earliest Eastern Orthodox icons of the Pentecost include Mary. By adding Mary, the Orthodox Church makes a theological statement about her inclusion in the church. Here, Mary is wearing the red and blue combination that we've seen on Jesus, except in reverse. Her blue interior is the cosmos from where Christ came, and the outer red garment is the earth-bound realm that receives him through her.

At the bottom of the icon is a small arch, inside an old king named Kosmos stands who represents the world. Kosmos is the Greek word meaning "world." His crown symbolizes earthly authority, i.e., he represents all the peoples of the world. He extends a cloth containing twelve scrolls representing the twelve tribes of Israel which continue with the teachings of the Apostles.

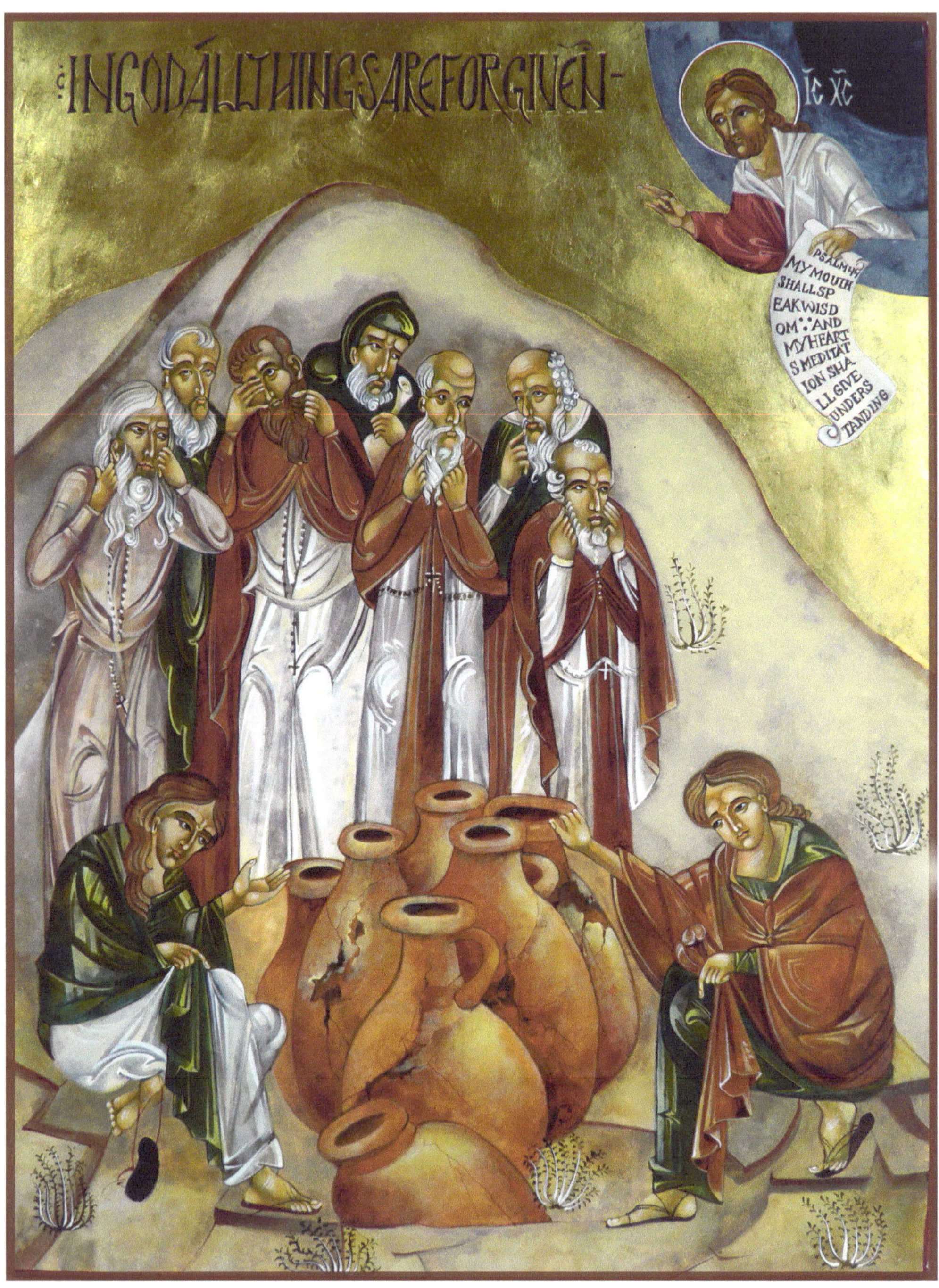
IN GOD ALL THINGS ARE FORGIVEN
IC XC
PSALM 49 MY MOUTH SHALL SPEAK WISDOM AND MY HEARTS MEDITATION SHALL GIVE UNDERSTANDING

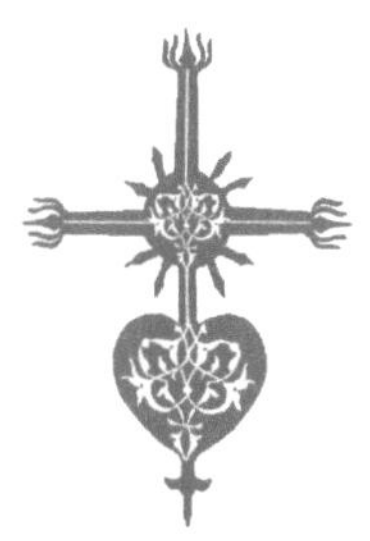

Cracked Pots and Confusion

The idea for this image, Crackpots and Confusion began as a day off, exhausted by listening to the news and thinking about lack of wholesome stewardship for our planet. God has much forgiveness and we in turn must develop it for one another.

I have been frustrated with humanity's inability to get along and be kind. There is plenty to learn and innumerable ways to do so. The cracked pots remind me of my mother who often used the term to describe situations driven by unpleasant people acting badly. She was clear about the sen- timent, sometimes we do not have the required info to influence anything yet continue to make noise. We become as useless as cracked pots.
The confusion is portrayed by all the men stoking their beards and looking confounded. It was group of learned men who formed the foundation of the church. Their heartfelt leadership and descendants has not always been inspired by wisdom or understanding. Humanity has not developed humility before God, and our noisy behavior of wants and demands is amplified every decade. The crescendo is deafening along with its destruction.

The two women at the bottom of the icon are looking at the seven cracked pots thinking about repairs or what to do in the wake of change. They represent the seven deadly sins.

Jesus speaks from above with the consoling words, "My mouth shall speak wisdom and my heart's meditation shall give understanding".

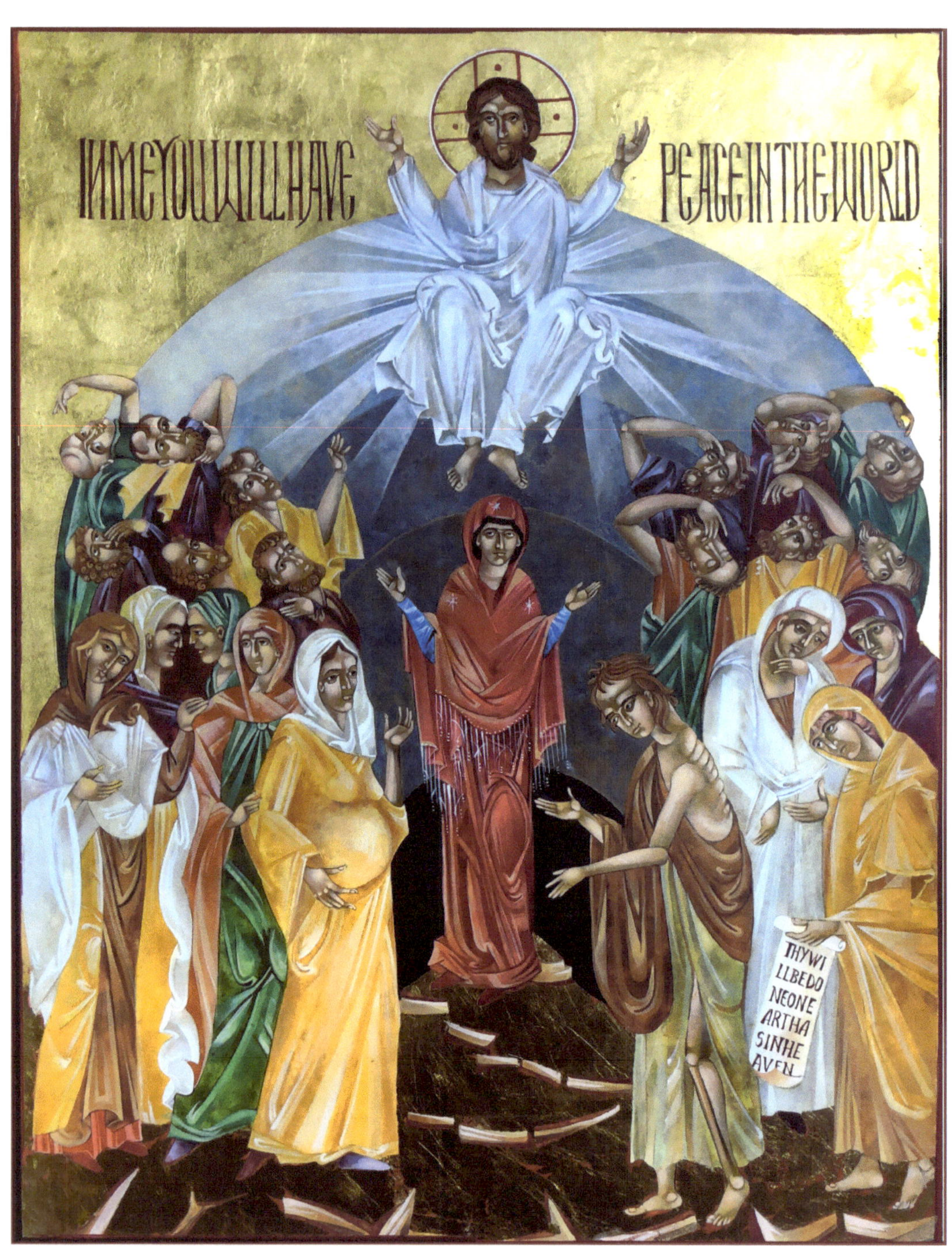
IN ME YOU WILL HAVE
PEACE IN THE WORLD
THY WI
LL BE DO
NE ONE
ARTHA
SINHE
AVEN

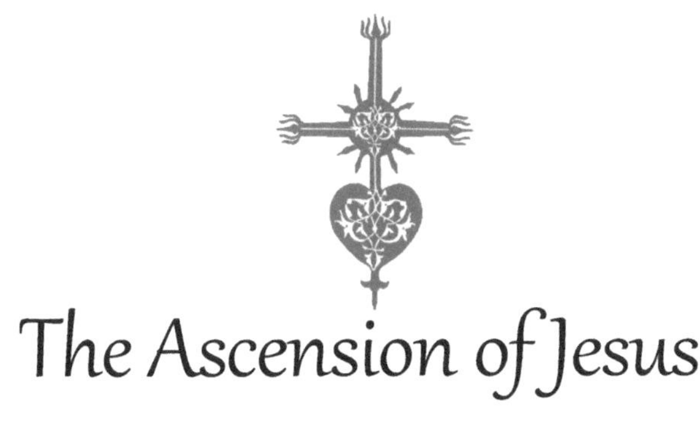

The Ascension of Jesus

"Jesus said, 'I am with you for only a short time, and then I am going to the one who sent me.'" Christ blesses the assembly with his right hand. He ascends, entrusting humankind with his living word and example of that word incarnate. The icon expresses with precision that Jesus is an example, guide, and source of inspiration for the church. He ascended into heaven, leaving us to figure out the significance of his life's work and message. Mary occupies the center of the icon and is placed directly below her son as he ascends. Her hands are extended in a gesture of prayer. Her calm presence is notably different from the appearance of the disciples.

The text reads "In me you will have peace in the World." More now than ever we need peace, his teaching asks us to turn the other cheek, to lay down our weapons and to love without fear of losing our selves. There is a tremendous amount of noise in the world as we work out how to understand, "Thy will be done on earth as in heaven."

Jesus's followers are agitated, talking to one another, looking and pointing- towards heaven. The contrast is a compelling representation of the church as we know it, often in disagreement and/or misunderstanding. The disciples appear to have questions and a lot of them. I find this icon to be like an unfinished story. This icon is curious. It raises questions. It shows the disciples are agitated. Scripture reveals their concern: what shall we do now?

Acts 1:9-11 "After he said this, he was taken up before their very eyes, and a cloud hid him from their sight. They were looking intently up into the sky as he was going, when suddenly two men dressed in white stood beside them. 'Men of Galilee,' they said, 'why do you stand here looking into the sky?' This same Jesus, who has been taken from you into heaven, will come back in the same way you have seen him go into heaven". His instruction has been given; we are now called to work it out among ourselves.

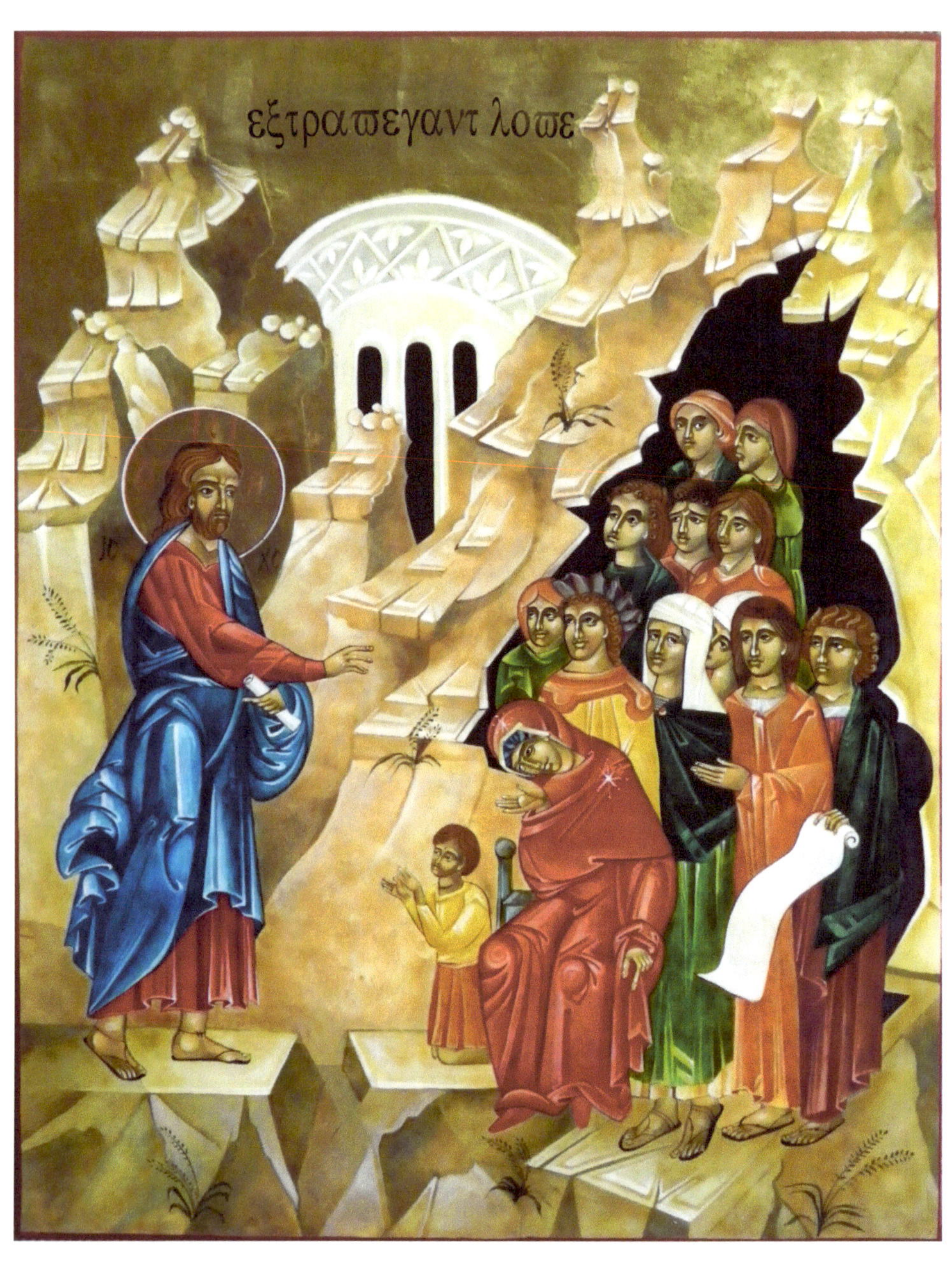

εξτραπεγαντ λοωε
IC XC

Jesus Appears to the Women

In this icon, eleven women and a little girl approach Christ out of the darkness as a community. The women are represented as disciples committed to learn and be taught by Christ. They are not concerned with authority but rather the His message. They will have to step across a small abyss which prevents them from being more included in the Christ story. The cracked ground they stand on is old dry earth, broken, and separated which hinders their communion.

The church has set them apart from the disciples named in the Bible, but women never stopped sharing their exemplary discipleship to comfort, strengthen, and instruct others with the wisdom they had learned from the same teacher.

Who are these women? Mary the mother of Jesus, Mary of Bethany, Mary, mother of John. Mary, wife of Cleopas, Mary Magdalene, Mary, the mother of James and wife of Clephas, Joanna, the wife of Chusa, who was steward to Herod Antipas, Salome, the mother of the sons of Zebedee, Suzanna, and Martha and Mary, the sisters of Lazarus. Seven Mary's out of eleven, we were not named properly.

These women mentioned have been witness to the empty tomb after the resurrection and had plenty of time to meditate on the instructions given by the Savior. They have lived and been tested in body, mind, and spirit, through the past, present, and future, in thy kingdom, thy will, and thy spirit. Yet, what we know of as Biblical text, divine words, and all inspired by God, have silenced them with texts like, "Let Women learn in silence with submissiveness. I permit no woman to teach or to have authority over men; she is to keep silent. For Adam was formed first and then Eve; and Adam was not deceived, but woman was deceived and became the transgressor. Yet woman will be saved through bearing children, if she continues in faith and love and holiness with modesty." (1 Tim 2:11-15) As a woman I find biblical texts like this infuriating and outdated!

WE ARE ALL CHILDREN OF GOD, ALL RECIPIENTS OF CREATION AND WE ARE CALLED TO LEARN, LOVE AND SHARE WHAT WE HOPE IS TRUTH.

About Us

Mary Jane Miller, born 1954 in New York has been a full-time artist and thinker her entire life, and dedicated to iconography for the past 30 years. She and her husband Valentin Gomez reside in San Miguel de Allende, Mexico. Their complete collection of narrative icons called Life in Christ is available in book form. The collection is for sale or by individual request in a limited addition. All the icons are original one-of-a-kind egg tempera paintings, 23 kt Gold and 100% pewter repoussé images. Valentin works in the repoussé technique and Mary Jane designs and paints. Our dream is to add a few more icons to those existing in the world, hoping that this great sacred art tradition will continue in liturgy and prayer for a long time to come. Miller's books are useful for individual devotions, to read as a bible study, sacred art reflections, a gift for your congregation or the church library.

OTHER PUBLISHED WORKS

In Light of Women her latest icon collection created as an exploration of women's image in iconography and their voices in the church. Vibrant text describing each images history, religious context and her own reflections about the world we live in today.

Icon Painting Technique, A Meditation and Guide to Egg Tempera explains the subtle relationship between the process of icon painting and how it reflects and enriches one's spiritual life.

The Mary Collection This collection of Mary icons captures the mysteries of the Madonna, drawing attention to the relationship between Mary and Christ, and the viewer. A wide range of imagination and potential is explored this tiny book.

Ancient Image, Sacred Lines and Coloring book for Women are collections of icon templates for painting and drawing. Each drawing is a meditation for healing or a template for iconographers. They are coloring books design with journal space to write down reflections.

Women in Iconography More women in Iconography a collection of 72 images from mystics and saints to rebels and thinkers. Not enough women are named in the bible yet the research and discovery is beginning. Perfect for women's studies. An additional study coloring book for women with templates for all the images.

BOOKS CAN BE PURCHASED ON LULU.COM AND AMAZON.COM.
AND WEBSITE SACREDICONRETREAT.COM

Mary Jane Miller has been steeped in the byzantine style egg tempera icon painting tradition since 1980. She says it is not easy to be driven by something you can't see, to become completely absorbed by a desire you're afraid to follow or ignore. In her studio, painting, patience and prayer are the everyday format. Iconographers live and work in a sort of double dimension where time and space are distorted, image and content change reality, and solitude speaks volumes. Miller and her spouse Valentin Gomez, are both self-taught and have been quietly working together for 50 years.

The technique and egg tempera medium enabled us to realize something quite intimate about God, that is, "we create as we are created". In their hearts all iconographers believe that "beauty will save the world". I believe that the act of icon painting transmits everything that is beautiful in humanity and a growing sense of the divine in all Creation.

Miller is quickly becoming a catalyst for change. The voices of women and female saints have not been sufficiently included in the church teachings. The contemporary commentary going on about Christian traditions and women is changing the landscape of religion and spirituality. Contemporary women have been waiting for over 2,000 years to be given an equal but different place in the kingdom. 'Men of God', it is time to teach and give guidance to bring Christ's directives of love and equality into fruition.

For more info about Mary Jane Miller

CLASSIC ICONOGRAPHY   HTTP://WWW.SANMIGUELICONS.COM/
WORKSHOPS OFFERE   HTTP://WWW.SACREDICONRETREAT.COM/
CNTEMPORARY ICONOGRAPHY   HTTPS://WWW.MILLERICONS.COM/

Peace be Still

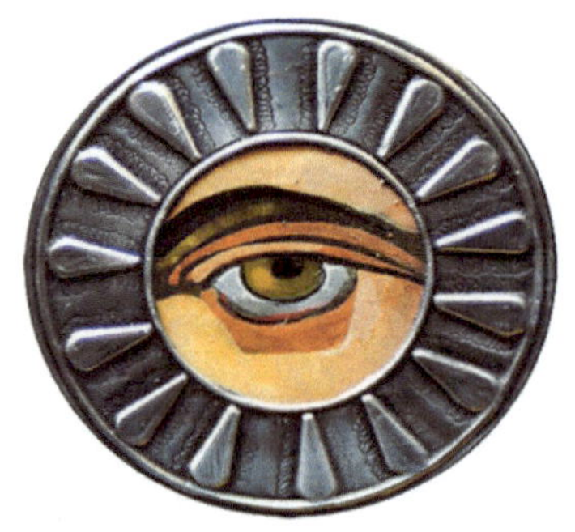